P9-CSH-434

DENNIS FRIEDMAN is a psychiatrist and the author of innovative studies of phobias, sexual problems and other psychological disorders. His previous works for Peter Owen are *Darling Georgie: The Enigma of King George V*, *Ladies of the Bedchamber: The Role of the Royal Mistress* and his first novel, *The Lonely Hearts Club*.

LINCOLN SELIGMAN is a painter, sculptor and illustrator. He has had numerous West End exhibitions and a one-man show of paintings at the Royal Academy, London. He has recently designed ballets for the New English Ballet Theatre at Sadler's Wells and at London's Royal Opera House.

By the same author

Darling Georgie: The Enigma of King George V (Peter Owen)
Ladies of the Bedchamber: The Role of the Royal Mistress (Peter Owen)
The Lonely Hearts Club (Peter Owen)
Inheritance: A Psychological History of the Royal Family
An Unsolicited Gift: Why We Do What We Do

Behind the
FACADE

A Psychiatrist's View

Dennis Friedman

With illustrations by
Lincoln Seligman

PETER OWEN
London and Chicago

PETER OWEN PUBLISHERS
81 Ridge Road, London N8 9NP

Peter Owen books are distributed in the USA and Canada by
Independent Publishers Group/Trafalgar Square
814 North Franklin Street, Chicago, IL 60610, USA

First published in Great Britain 2013 by
Peter Owen Publishers

© Dennis Friedman 2013

Illustrations and cover image © Lincoln Seligman 2013

All rights reserved.
No part of this publication may be reproduced in any form or by any
means without written permission of the publishers.

ISBN 978-0-7206-1507-4

A catalogue record for this book is available from
the British Library

Typeset by Octavo-Smith Ltd in Constantia 10.5/14
www.octavosmith.com

Printed and bound in the UK by
CPI Group (UK) Ltd, Croydon, CR0 4YY

For my wife Rosemary, my four beautiful daughters
and my ten grandchildren

CONTENTS

Introduction	9
Unhappy Birthday	21
The Memory Bench	27
Two for Tea	33
Ball Game	39
Bell, Book and Candle	43
Crowning Glory	51
Chequered	57
Silver Service	65
A Good Seat	69
Lethal	73
Near You	77
Talion Law	79
Timetable	83
Ticker	89
Apology	93
Aspiration	97
Cat's Eyes	103
Ides	107
The Milkman	111
Appetite	119
Each-Way Bet	123
Jam on It	129
Fully Booked	135
Mama Mia	139
Time Warp	145

On the Cards	151
Tim Whittington	155
Caught You	161
It's My Body	165
Noli Me Tangere	169
Busy Body	173
Sexploitation	179
Damned Spot	185
Pull Yourself Together	189

INTRODUCTION

'Things are not necessarily lovely behind the facade,
and so it is with human beings too.' – Sigmund Freud

PATIENTS SOMETIMES ASK why I do what I do. It is a good
question, and I usually tell them, 'Curiosity.' This generally
brings the conversation to an end. Although most patients are
probably thinking about their reasons for becoming a patient,
rather than mine for becoming a psychiatrist, the question
hints at a reluctance to get down to business, at worries about
dependency and at an unwillingness to give up control.
Discussing personal problems with someone you have only
just met is never easy.

The initial assessment may also be difficult for the therapist,
so help is always welcome. Non-verbal clues can be picked up
from the moment the patient rings the bell. Is she early or late?
If early, is she hoping that you will have more time with her and
for her? If late, is it because she's dragging her feet about
therapy or because she cannot bear to be kept waiting? Is the
doorbell ring long and assertive or short and timid? What is her
handshake like? Is it firm and confident or flabby and clammy?
And what does she do with her coat? She has the option of
flinging it on to the sofa – making herself at home – or hanging
it on the coat stand. When she begins to speak further clues

emerge. 'I don't have a problem, doctor. It's my husband.' Defences such as denial may sometimes be temporarily helpful in coping with issues such as bereavement, which might otherwise be unmanageable. But they will soon need to be addressed, because they conceal problems and make them more difficult to confront.

Once the patient and I have discovered what the problem is and why she has hung on to it, the first step towards resolving it will have been taken. She will come to see that although her symptom may have been understandable in its original situation, usually in childhood, it no longer is. She will then find it easier later to abandon it using the 'here and now' techniques of cognitive behavioural therapy.

Well, why did I become a psychiatrist and not a patient, since both are concerned with problem behaviour? I soon realized that everyone has problems of one sort or another, but it goes without saying that if the psychiatrist has not resolved his own issues he will be unable to help his patients resolve theirs.

Even as a child I think I must have suspected that there was a lot going on that I needed to know about. I would have reacted at the time to the attitudes of those around me. Although I did not know it then, problems can often be diverted into something useful. My problem was curiosity, and I was able to divert it into finding out, into research, into discovery. Whenever my mother told me to do something I would usually ask what she meant. I was what she called 'inquisitive'. 'Always asking questions,' she would say. 'You'll probably be a detective when you grow up.' She was right. 'Making enquiries' has always interested me. Nothing is ever quite what it appears to be. It's not what's written on the tin that is important; it is what's *not* written on it.

Long before I graduated from medical school I wondered about what people did not say. 'Wait until your father comes home,' my mother's favourite threat, often led not to the retribution, which in the heat of the moment she had probably planned, but to anticipatory anxiety in me. By the time my father had returned from work my mother usually felt sorry for me and forgot to tell him. There might have been other things on her mind – pity or protectiveness – but I did not know what they were. Should she have told me how she really felt? Neither of us would have been aware that she had used pity as a defence against her wish to punish me, but we might both have benefited from discussing it.

What struck me much later, while I was working as a doctor in general practice, was that patients who seemed to come for problems they might quite easily have allowed to resolve spontaneously usually had other agendas. They needed someone to listen to them. Had they also been kept in the dark about their mothers' feelings? I soon realized that their presenting symptoms were sometimes just the tip of the iceberg. If I had given them a moment or two would they have told me what was really troubling them? I don't think so. Even then I knew that they would need longer than that.

If my unconscious was speaking to me when I graduated sixty-four years ago I was not listening to it. I should have been thinking about my career, but I had recently married and thought I knew where my priorities lay. Promising to stay with someone until 'death did us part' was not the rather loose arrangement it has become for many. Commitment was a serious matter, and I had to put my mind to it. I did not know then that commitment was a 'birth' gift from one's mother and that her ability to build an understanding with her child based on love and trust would years later become an essential ingredient in another loving partnership.

There were several work options available. Specialized training, involving a slow climb up a hospital ladder, was one, but I had my wife to support and was keen to start work immediately. I liked people, and I liked listening. I decided to try my hand at general practice. After working for a while as a house physician and then as a casualty officer I joined a single-handed practice on the edge of a housing estate run by an elderly Scotsman. I was taken on as his assistant. He would train me, he said. The NHS had recently been introduced, and delivery of health care had reinvented itself. The biggest change was that medical attention was now free at the point of need. It took me a while to realize that the prescriptions for cotton wool and bandages everyone was demanding were not for the treatment of minor injuries but for stuffing cushions and making lampshades. I learned very little else from my employer, because he had learned little since being granted a licence to practise some time before the Diamond Jubilee of Queen Victoria. He did not believe in sterilization, often smoked on the rare occasions when he actually examined a patient and immunized babies against diphtheria using a syringe that he kept in the ashtray on his desk. He believed, however, that he was at the forefront of modern medicine. Vaccination against smallpox was in full swing, and at last women were not being discouraged from taking advantage of hospital obstetrics with its emphasis on antisepsis and antenatal care. They would once have been, because he would have been paid an extra fee for delivering their children at home.

I enjoyed solving mysteries, and forensic curiosity was a character trait that I had not realized I possessed. I remember thinking that I could have joined the police force – as my mother had suggested – or even taken up crime writing. Years later I had a patient whose sole ambition at the time was to 'get away with murder'. When she finally gave up trying to persuade men – usually ones married to someone else – to have an affair with her she sublimated her urges into something more creative and became a successful crime writer, always ensuring that the criminal would be apprehended and justice done.

Each of my surgeries would go on for hours, partly because there were very few patients but mainly because I enjoyed listening to people's problems. I would like to say that this might have been why I became a psychiatrist, but it probably was not. It was that people found it easy to talk to me. It was not so much that they were looking for answers, although they did not know it – for which I was grateful at the time, since I had few to give them – they just wanted to be heard. 'You're not listening' is possibly one of the first whole sentences a child addresses to a parent. To be listened to is a need that probably switches on at birth and remains switched on throughout life. A baby's every cry has a specific meaning, and it is a happy child whose mother understands their significance. However much children need to be heard, and however much their parents hope they will always be available to deal with their needs, it is seldom the case that each cry is attended to appropriately. I have come to realize that sometimes children have to grow up first. Then if they become patients in therapy they might get their needs met.

During my early days at school I recall a strong urge to know what was happening around me. The books I read for pleasure came under the heading of adventure and exploration and were written specifically for schoolboys. *Tom Brown's Schooldays*, *Treasure Island* and *Robinson Crusoe* were particular favourites. I also read every William book by Richmal Crompton several times. It was important for me to know how William – my *alter ego* – coped with the many difficulties that arose in his life. He was constantly in trouble, but self-help, being told to pull himself together and parental wrath seemed to be all that was on offer. I would love to have known what happened to William when he grew up, but his fictional life seemed to end when he was fourteen. I did not know it then, but I know it now: no one ever grows up; they just grow older. I have often wondered whether wanting to know what happened to people after they were fourteen has been the real motive for my interest in people's motivations and feelings.

I had no idea during the 1930s that we were about to experience terrible times. One of the most momentous events of my childhood was the arrival in London in 1938 of Sigmund Freud accompanied by William Bullitt, the American ambassador to Paris, and the psychoanalyst Princess Marie Bonaparte. The circumstances of his arrival as a refugee in Britain signalled the inhumanity to which so many people, one way or another, were to become exposed. One of the great intellects of the time, virtually at the end of his life, had arrived to make a fresh start in a country far from home and without any of the accoutrements that had decorated and substantiated his thinking. He was without his books and his papers, and his research and his memories – bewildered by illness and catastrophic prejudice – were being trampled on by savages in Vienna. Later, one of my most treasured possessions was a brief letter to my grandmother from Professor Freud. From his new home in Hampstead he wrote that he was sorry to be unable to help her daughter, my aunt, because he was too ill. I still have the letter.

Freud's shock discovery that everyone had secret sexual desires was a common topic of dinner-table conversation. His work, translated into English by Ernest Jones, was readily available and written in a literary style that had earned the author the Goethe Prize for Literature in 1930. English society did not know what to make of Freud's theories, but that did not prevent them from discussing them to demonstrate how broad-minded they were. The literati were just on the verge of shaking off Victorian prudery, but social change was in the air.

My mother's sister, who was well ahead of her time in her thinking and of whom I was very fond, took me everywhere. She was an historian and biographer, and accompanying her one evening to a book launch in an apartment in Park Lane I became so carried away by the excitement of being in the company of writers, actors and playwrights that I made a social gaffe. Encouraged by my aunt I may have had a few sips of champagne, but I can find no excuse for forgetting not only where I was but who I was. The nation was still mourning the death of King George V. The grave daily bulletins posted on the gates of Buckingham Palace at midnight ensured the population's concern for the monarch's health. They were signed by Lord Dawson of Penn and Lord Horder, physicians to the Royal Family who had impressed themselves on His Majesty's subjects by their use of language equalled only by that of Winston Churchill during the world war to follow.

I was taken aback when my aunt said to a man standing next to her, 'I must introduce my nephew to you. He's going to be a doctor one day.' The man held out his hand to greet me, and I put my rather smaller and certainly clammier hand into that of Lord Horder himself, committing a solecism that I have never forgotten. Instead of saying 'How do you do, sir?' I said, 'How are you?'

'Very kind of you to enquire about my health,' Lord Horder replied, affronted, before turning away. What I think I learned from that incident was that everyone needs to feel acknowledged, even the most illustrious figures, and that greeting Lord Horder as if he was one of my schoolmates made him uncomfortable. I had looked up at him, and he had been looking down at me. Did he feel somehow diminished by my failure to greet him appropriately? I certainly felt diminished by his implied reprimand. It was a lesson I never forgot.

My schooldays passed in a flash, and now I only remember the highlights. But life as a medical student was more memorable mainly because of the consultant who headed the Department of Psychological Medicine at my teaching hospital. Dr Eric Strauss was by far the most influential and charismatic of my teachers. Never without a cigarette while lecturing and forever coughing, the effect he had on my thinking has never left me. He was the first to make me feel that we, as students, were dealing with real people rather than with a collection of mental health problems. The concept of 'lunatics in asylums' was fast fading, but there was as yet very little available therapeutically other than addictive amphetamines and barbiturates and electro-convulsive therapy for patients at large in the community. Many of those he introduced to us were people of our own age. We found it easy to identify with them and to understand how they felt and how we might feel were we to suffer similar problems. We were impressed with Dr Strauss's efforts to restore those with mental illness to society, with his intellect and with his ability to help us comprehend how people might feel in adverse circumstances. He told us how, while serving on the Western Front in the First World War and suffering from shell-shock, he was often so terrified that he would vomit before going into battle. He was an expert on comparative religion and a practising Catholic. His attitude to mental health was eclectic. Through his friendship with Carl Jung and his association with the views of Freud's contemporary Alfred Adler, we came to understand that there was more to mental illness than had previously been comprehended. Eric Strauss introduced me to my feelings. I was sad to hear a few years later that he had died – not from lung cancer but from another smoking-related illness, coronary artery disease. I was intrigued to hear that on his deathbed he had given up his Catholic faith and returned to Judaism, the religion of his mother. He had given us much to ponder on *pre mortem*. I little thought it would continue *post mortem*.

I cannot say that Eric Strauss was solely responsible for my undergoing a five-year Kleinian analysis while I was giving up general practice, since major changes in life are usually multi-factorial. What I did learn from him was not to be rigid and that there was always another way. Strauss found his other way in religion. I found my other way in therapy. The antithesis to analysis, where what has gone before is seminal, is behaviour therapy in which what is going on now is thought by some to have the greater therapeutic significance.

During my analysis I found time to absorb the principles of the behavioural approach and had developed a method of treating anxiety that worked well in the treatment of single-object phobias, such as the fear of mice and spiders. I later extended this method to include claustrophobia and agoraphobia, conditions concerned with commitment. It involved presenting the feared situation in imagination to the patient, who was prevented from reacting with anxiety to it by inducing a state of relaxation using a short-acting intravenous barbiturate.

Another aspect of the behavioural approach that interested me was its use in sexual dysfunction. While working as a lecturer in the Department of Psychological Medicine at St Bartholomew's Hospital I was asked by its then Head of Department, Professor Linford Rees, to set up a sexual dysfunction clinic. In 1948 sexual problems had been demystified by the research work of Alfred Kinsey, a zoologist at the University of Indiana, and later by the sex therapists W.H. Masters and V.E. Johnson at the Institute of Human Sexuality in St Louis, Missouri. Men and women no longer felt that they had to put up with performance anxiety. Many men, otherwise fit and healthy, who suffered from erectile difficulty were inhibiting their normal responses through a fear of failing to live up to what they believed were their partners' expectations of them. Similar anxieties occurred in women who were unable to achieve orgasm. By employing the technique used to treat phobic anxiety, patients with sexual anxiety were taught to relax in the imagined presence of the anxiety-provoking situation. Within a few sessions they were able to transfer the relaxed feelings induced in them in therapy to the feared situation. While it was clearly important to relieve a distressing symptom, erectile difficulty was seldom a straightforward problem and was often a harbinger of marital disaster. Both partners suffer the effects of it, and one or other of them may decide to take the problem elsewhere. When others become involved the problem can take on another dimension. Difficulties may arise when one partner fails to interpret correctly the body language of the other, while verbal communication may also break down.

It is in this area of unrealistic expectation, misunderstanding and confusion, when partners cease to speak the same language as one another, that analytic therapy and behavioural therapy finally meet. Nowhere is this more physically obvious than in the sexual apathy that may affect one or other partner after childbirth. Unresolved problems with the opposite-sex parent may reappear when a child is born. A man may scapegoat his wife (or a woman her husband) if either is reminded of early problems with his or her opposite-sex parent. Finding themselves in bed with a parent, even if they are aware that it is the parent of their child rather than their own parent, may activate the incest taboo. An analytic approach will illuminate the problem, and a behavioural technique may be required to remove the imagined parent from between them in the marital bed.

It was at this time that I was faced with a patient who had a problem that highlighted the value of the behavioural approach. A nightwatchman on a building site was suffering from a dog phobia. His employer had insisted that the site have extra protection at night and took on an aggressive Alsatian. The nightwatchman, profoundly deaf and unable to speak, was terrified. He was in danger of losing his job and stood little chance of getting another. He could not tell me how he felt, and any advice from me would, quite literally, fall on deaf ears. A talking therapy was plainly inappropriate. Focusing on the symptom and ignoring whatever underlying cause there was for his phobia, I cut out pictures of dogs from magazines, ranging from cuddly puppies to a ferocious Rottweiler. These pictures frightened him, but he was prevented from experiencing panic by an injection of an ultra-short-acting barbiturate which induced relaxation in him while he looked at them. The desensitization process transferred to the feared situation, and within a few weeks his fear of dogs had virtually disappeared.

There will always be certain disorders where a behavioural approach will be the treatment of choice. The nightwatchman is an obvious example. An analytic approach, allowing the patient as long as it takes to get over a painful early memory which is continuing to make its presence felt years later, will sooner rather than later benefit from a therapeutic version of the admonition to 'get over it'. A combination of both techniques is, I believe, the treatment of choice. No one really wants to continue living in a past that was seldom happy. Moving on and letting go of it is essential. Understanding the past is fundamental to understanding the present. But, once understood, the compulsion to live in it may be discouraged by the use of a cognitive approach.

I have been privileged to have many people share their feelings with me over the years. In many ways it is a selfish privilege in that it is invariably one way. People with problems are anyway more interested in their own feelings than they are in mine – and it is right that they should be. Long after their therapy has ended they may, however, wonder what I would say about other issues they may be confronting. If these issues evoke an echo of earlier discussions so much the better. Getting the old game plan out of the cupboard and giving it a dust down may be all that's needed. The patient will know what to do.

Behind the Facade is a collage of my case studies presented as short stories in the interests of confidentiality. They are inspired by some of the problems with which I have had to deal during my working life. Some emphasize the effects of mothering on the way adults interact with one another. Others focus on the father's role after the infant has been weaned. All illustrate how an unhappy adult may find the means to move on to leading a tolerant and happy life rather than persisting with an angry and miserable one.

UNHAPPY BIRTHDAY

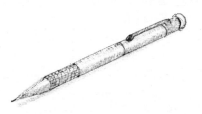

S HE HATED THE dull grey December afternoons. Waiting out-side school invariably evoked memories of being forgotten, of being abandoned. Gideon had just started nursery school, and every afternoon was a never-changing routine; the same people, the same conversation, the same banter, the same looking out for Gideon's friend Frankie. It was a club. Anyone could join. Membership depended only on having been procreative.

She thought of her birthday and wondered why Roger had not planned on taking her out for dinner to celebrate it. But he had bought her a present. It was a thoughtful one, but there was something about it that made her feel uneasy. It was not as if he had forgotten her birthday. That really would have worried her. It was the superior old-fashioned propelling pencil bearing a strange coat of arms that was the problem. What puzzled her was why he had chosen to give her a pencil in the first place. Had he bought her a new computer that would have been a different matter. The pencil looked expensive. It might even have been a collector's item. Roger was meticulous about presents and would have given it a good deal of thought. She might have understood his choice better had he not been aware that their home was littered with pencils. None of them were smart-looking nor propelling; common-or-garden pencils you would not be too bothered about were you to lose them. Like the pizzas they often ordered, they were takeaways or throwaways. There were always more where they came from.

She was not into pencils – particularly those that were more show horse than work horse. She was interested only in what could be written with them. The idea of a pencil as an ornament irritated her. He was not usually insensitive. He knew her almost as well as she knew herself. She decided to delete that thought. She did not like the look of it. She was interested only in how so many thoughts were visual rather than cerebral. At least they were for poets.

There were six pencils on her desk and jars of them in every room. That there were never enough was certainly true. Despite their proliferation they could be hard to find in a hurry, such as when a telephone callback was needed; she knew she would never remember eleven numbers. But it was more than that. When an idea for a poem came to her she had to make a note of it at once. If she didn't pin it down it would flutter away like a butterfly, never to be recaptured. It was he who had taught her how ephemeral ideas could be, how easily they might be lost.

Poetry was a passion they shared: he in his love of it, she in her writing of it. She had been twice shortlisted for the Bridport Prize in the last five years. She was a poet; not a pencil collector. Was there something defensive in that? She knew he took her achievements seriously because he loved and admired her. It was he who had encouraged her to commit her thoughts and feelings to paper in the first place. Communication was important to him, although it was not poetry but music that he spoke. The clarinet was his pride and joy. He had only recently bought a new one. Its bass voice was different from its predecessor, and it was extra long. Not unlike the pencil he had bought her.

She knew him well enough to know that he would have chosen something he thought she wanted, something that had meaning for her or perhaps – she thought suddenly – meaning for him. Was he sending her an encrypted message? Was he trying to tell her something? She had no idea. That pencils were phallic and were expected to have lead in them was too obvious, a cliché he would have dismissed.

If there was a hidden message in his gift, or if there was something bothering him, he should have discussed it with her. She wanted to be rid of her strange feeling. She was becoming obsessed with it. She had thanked him, but that did not relieve her anxiety. Feelings of guilt drifted through her mind. Had she done something to account for how she felt? Had she committed an offence? She began to sift through her memories. Her wickedness list had very little on it. Had her worries more to do with an earlier time? When she had misbehaved as a child her parents would never reprimand her but would instead give her disapproving looks. She had never forgotten those looks, which had been left to her to interpret. She seldom knew what she had done wrong, and she did not know now, but whenever she thought of them feelings of guilt would flood back. She would have liked to explore her memory more thoroughly, but she was too worried to think about anything other than the ornate pencil. She looked at it again more closely, examining it, rolling it around her fingers, weighing it up, waiting for it to speak. It remained mute. It did not look at her disapprovingly. She felt as if she was assessing a find in a junk shop and wondered whether she would pick up vibes that might encourage her to make an offer. But there were no vibes.

Why couldn't she accept the pencil for what it was? It was a pencil. Did there have to be a hidden agenda? Why not just accept it graciously? It had a nice feel to it, and it was beginning to settle in her hand as if taking up residence, feeling at home. Sometimes a pencil was just a pencil. She was not entirely sure what Freud had meant when he said that sometimes a cigar is just a cigar. Well, she *was* sure but did not want to think about it. Not all Freud's theories had stood the test of time. Whatever they may once have symbolized cigars now meant only lung cancer. She looked again at the pencil. The shape was interesting and almost familiar. It reminded her of something. It was neither gold nor silver – it was only her thirty-fifth birthday after all – but it was certainly handsome. Given time she might take to it, although she knew nothing of its provenance, nothing about where in her husband's thinking it might have originated, only that he wanted her to have it. She tried to write her name, but it had no lead. She must tell him. Perhaps she was not meant to write with it, merely deduce something from it that he may have thought amusing; he had always been a joker. But a birthday was not a day for jokes. It was a day for memories, although no one, other than a mother, actually remembered a person's 'birth' day. A friend at college had sent his mother a card and flowers on *his* birthday. The card thanked her for giving him life and the flowers were because he loved her. Not funny. A bit spooky? Was the pencil to remind her of an event similarly seminal and equally unfunny? What was he trying to tell her? His messages were not usually coded. Perhaps they had been, but she had never thought to decode them. She began to worry. She was not brave enough to ask him whether there was a problem that neither knew about or if there was something wrong between them that he did not wish to address.

Confrontation made her nervous. He had been a bit odd lately. Now and then he would say something that would frighten her. She had even wondered if he had gone off her. They still had sex, but it was nothing like it used to be, although, come to think of it, it had never been brilliant. Of recent months it had been less passionate, less playful. He *had* remembered her birthday, which reassured her but only slightly.

Her thoughts went back to their wedding day seven years ago. She recalled every moment. Everything was new, brand new, untouched, virginal. She smiled. Not entirely true. He could hardly have expected that. She was twenty-eight. She had sex more than once with a fellow student, in fact, almost every day for a whole term. He had enjoyed it more than she did. At the time she had put it down to his technique. Maybe he had not tried hard enough to please her. But what did please her? She had never wanted to play the games in which he had tried to interest her. Did she think recreational sex was faintly unattractive? Was it only procreation that was acceptable? She did not want to think about it. She had not liked the student enough at the time to discuss what she now realized were her ever-present feelings of slight distaste. Anyway, it was embarrassing. It was still embarrassing even with someone with whom she had lived for seven years. But she preferred to think that it had something to do with her college friend, with whom she had been 'going out'. She hated that expression. It was so coy, so something not to be spoken of openly, so uptight. Was that how she was? He had been too earthy. Earthy was not something she was keen on. She was not even sure what she meant by earthy, but there was something unromantic about it. She wondered whether sex could ever be romantic. Dressing it up changed it from what it was. Pheromones disguised with perfume, locations switched from bedrooms to back seats of cars with fear of discovery adding extra arousal. That was it. It was the extra arousal that removed the earthiness from it and made it attractive. There was a time, it was after their child was born, that they had seemed really to settle down together. She was busy with the baby, he with his music. They were happy. They made few physical demands of one another.

Frankie's father reminded her of Roger. He was of similar build and similar age. He was the only male at the school gates. She wanted to ask him why Frankie's mother never came. Were they divorced? Did she want to know? Sometimes her thoughts made her blush. Every day she looked anxiously to see whether her thoughts made him blush. That they never seemed to do so disappointed her.

Gideon and Frankie held hands while they waited to be collected. They cried when they were taken their separate ways. Frankie's dad said, 'Why don't you bring Gideon to tea with Frankie?' She had manipulated him without uttering a word. He wrote down his address and mobile number on a slip of paper. He had an ornate pencil. The coat of arms was identical to that on hers.

'My desk partner, the clarinet player in the wind section, gave it to me. It is one of only two ever made.' Then she thought she heard him say so quietly that he seemed to be speaking only to himself, 'He and I make very good music together.' She shut her eyes for a long moment. When she opened them again the street lights had come on.

THE MEMORY BENCH

THERE WERE VERY few people in the park that morning. It was not an outdoor day, even for those who might have a date with destiny. A dog walker in the distance and two keep-fitters jogging, possibly more to keep warm than for reasons connected with health, came and went. A thin scattering of overnight snow added sparkling highlights to frozen spikes of grass as wintery sunshine shone briefly upon them. It was desperately cold, but Chatterton and his friend George, huddling together on their bench in their ancient army-officers' greatcoats, did not notice it. They had been friends since their student days at Cambridge, although neither found the company of the other particularly agreeable. Their conversations had become too predictable. But there were no others with whom they could share feelings or memories. All their friends were dead. Almost everyone they had ever known was dead. Neither of them had married. They had one sibling between them. They lived in the same care home and shared a common past. Their memories, their mobile phones and their bench were the links in the chain that bound them to one another.

Chatterton was talking. George was thinking, but in the interests of their friendship pretending to listen. They stared ahead, not into the future – they had no future – but into the deserted, decaying, manufactured landscape of the park. They were part of that landscape, dying with it, becoming colder with it, waiting with it as the once colourful but now dead summer bedding waited as it slowly decayed into compost that might one day nourish another generation waiting for its moment in the sun.

Suddenly, introspection on hold, they focused on an elderly cyclist wobbling towards them as he crossed the 'No Cycling' message painted clearly on the footpath in large white letters. He stopped near their bench. Chatterton was compelled, as always, to draw attention to misdemeanours however minor, provided they were not his own. Offended by the elderly cyclist's assault on the sense of order impressed upon him by his upbringing, he broke off from thoughts of his boarding-school, seventy years earlier, which he had tagged to become the next topic of conversation, believing incorrectly that George almost certainly would find these reminiscences of interest.

'You do know that cycling is illegal in the park?' he barked at the intruder.

His voice, once authoritative and now deteriorated into an almost inaudible quavering, had no obvious effect on the cyclist who, dismounting slowly and with difficulty, dropped his bicycle on to the frosty grass and lurched towards them. Regarding the stranger warily, both George and Chatterton thought anxiously of other threats long passed, student brawls outside pubs, clambering drunkenly over college walls to evade disciplinary proctors, more recently being mugged at cashpoints. They were no longer accustomed to strangers approaching them with who-knows-what in mind. These days it could be so much more than the offensive finger or its abusive verbal equivalent. Taking the wind out of their sails, the elderly cyclist asked politely whether George and Chatterton would mind moving up a bit because he wanted to sit down. The two men looked at one another. No other bench as far as their misty eyes could see had anyone sitting on it. But they were relieved. Confrontation seemed not to be a problem.

Chatterton was not really concerned about cycling in the park. He cared only about two things: the importance of authority and his past life – about which, as they sat on their bench, he spoke *ad nauseam* to George. Shifting reluctantly an inch or two sideways they made room for the elderly white-haired man who probably had not heard what Chatterton had said about cycling in the park and who might even have mistaken his admonition for a greeting. Looked at more closely, he clearly could not have posed a threat either to them or to anyone else. Smiling and with a friendly wave of the hand he said, 'Jelly. Conrad Jelly. Known as Wobbly.' After a moment or two, and in the absence of any kind of reaction from either of his recently acquired companions, he began speaking as if he had known them for years. The impression he gave was that he had begun talking some time earlier, then broken off for a while and was now carrying on where he had left off.

'I was a boarder at the time,' he said, looking first at Chatterton and then at George and, in a quietly confiding tone, continued, 'I was a new boy. I must have been about eleven. The headmaster was a tyrant. He used to tell everyone that I was called Jelly because I was wobbly. Most distressing. Thought he was being funny. Could have meant wobbly intellectually, although I thought he meant wobbly on my feet. I was not in the habit of falling over, but I do have to say that at the time I did not feel entirely on firm ground. My real name was Jellinek, a Czech name. My father thought it too foreign. We had not long been in England. Although his English was good it was obviously not good enough to understand that Jelly was not a name with which to saddle a child. I was stuck with Wobbly.'

Chatterton's reaction to their new companion was not what George was expecting. Often embarrassingly aggressive, his friend possessed neither social graces nor diplomacy but frequently spouted dogma, prejudice and racist comments to which George seldom listened.

For the first time in his life Chatterton had nothing to say. It felt to George as if it was 11 a.m. on Armistice Day. Two minutes of blissful silence, two minutes without auditory bombardment. Chatterton was staring, rather oddly George thought, at their new companion, unconscious that they might be experiencing similar feelings. Chatterton did not try to express his emotions and seemed unaware that Mr Jelly might be experiencing the same. He saw only an old man, of similar age to his own, and felt that he was looking not at a stranger but into a mirror, reflecting not himself but images of a time long passed.

Falteringly and in a voice unlike his usual aggressive one, wishing perhaps to echo the voice of his new friend, he held out his hand and said, 'Chatterton. Like yours it's a nickname. I was also given it at school.' He paused, wondering why he wanted to tell a stranger what he had kept to himself for a lifetime. Was it because he was a stranger? Was it all right for old men to divulge lifelong secrets to other old men on park benches? He had always considered park benches to be for the exchange of memories but for selected memories only. Many of the seats bore memorial plaques. If anyone cared to remember him – which he doubted – he could be due for a bench of his own soon. Glancing briefly at George he decided that relying on him to provide a memorial would be a waste of time.

'I was almost five when I was asked my name at my primary school. I did not reply because I did not know it. Because I remained silent the teacher thought it amusing to refer to me as Chatterton, a kinder version of Chatterbox. I kept that name as an act of defiance. I don't know whom I'm defying. Maybe it was my mother, who if she spoke to me at all probably never addressed me by my name. Perhaps it was not the custom at the time to do so. I don't know. I know it's all nonsense now, but I've never really got over it. Defiance was not the done thing in those days. No one cares now. But it did make me feel a bit better when I tried it. Chatterton, not my real name, came with me to my public school where speaking in class was considered a serious offence. The penalty was to write lines. It was usually 'Silence Is Golden / Only Monkeys Chatter' fifty times, and a hundred times for a repeat offence. Silence is not golden, of course, and endless repetition of it taught me nothing. Speaking is a talent that should be nurtured not punished. It was years before I came to realize that I had been put into a double bind. I was demeaned by my teachers because they had not taken the trouble to discover who I was and had given me a label, Chatterton, that implied I had a lot to say for myself, then penalized me whenever I said it.'

Mr Jelly was listening, and Chatterton was chattering. A lifetime of having to struggle for his true voice to be heard had inexplicably disappeared.

Mr Jelly and Chatterton had clearly taken to one another. George sensed the change in his friend. The bench was small. They were bulky in their winter clothing and huddling together could lead to love or hate. It was too early to decide. George smiled to himself and then stopped. No one was smiling at him. On the contrary, Chatterton, who until the arrival of Mr Jelly had always faced him on the seat, now had his back turned. Formerly an insider, George had suddenly become an outsider. His listener role had been stolen. For the first time in years he felt angry. How about me? he asked himself. Nobody had ever encouraged him to tell his story. Was it because his impoverished childhood could not compare with that of a child growing up not knowing who he was, or now having to compete with a foreigner with a ridiculous name? And if he had a story why had he not revealed it to the only person left in his world who might listen? And why was he thinking like this now?

He repeated the question to himself, although he knew the answer. He remembered it as clearly as if it were yesterday, although it was over eighty years ago. It was the moment when his mother, his best friend and the only person he could speak to, the only person in whom he could confide, who understood and loved him, had suddenly left him. It was a day he would not forget. He was six, but it was as if it had just happened. He remembered how his father had looked that day, his face and his tears as he tried to help his son understand that although he would never see his mother again she had left them a baby brother who would always remind them of her. His father had promised that he would look after him and love him just as his mother had. But he had lied. He had turned his back on him and loved his baby brother instead.

He knew now why he could not tell anyone his story, not even on the memory bench, particularly not on the memory bench. It was a story of betrayal that had coloured his life, making him unable to communicate properly because of his anger. He remembered the rage that he had turned in on himself because he could not direct it towards his mother. She had died for him. She had provided him with the experience of brotherly love. But he had never loved his brother. She had died in vain.

Did this explain his lifelong depression and his inability to trust men? And his inability to trust women for fear they would abandon him? It was a life wasted, a life sentence self-inflicted. He had done nothing to deserve it. Was it happening again? He thought not. It had merely unlocked a door that he had himself slammed shut. He looked at Mr Jelly and at Chatterton chattering away. They had found one another, but he had found himself.

TWO FOR TEA

GABRIEL AND VALENTINA decided on a picnic for Sunday lunch. It was the tail end of August and almost everyone they knew was abroad or away in the country. Being Sunday there was not much to get up for. Even the shops didn't open until twelve. But Gabriel and Valentina did have somewhere to go. Their routine seldom changed. Sunday was their day for walking in the park, for commenting on the roses (there was a floribunda called Always Love You which made them smile whenever they came across it) and for ending up in the café for coffee before returning home to cook lunch. Today was special, however. It was Valentina's birthday.

They had just woken up. Valentina shut her eyes again, pretending to be asleep. It was a birthday ritual. She knew exactly what Gabriel was doing. He was stretching out his hand to reach for her card, which he had hidden under the bed the night before. Not looking at Gabriel added to the expected *frisson* of surprise. Much emphasis was laid on remembering. Both had had bad experiences of forgetting, when collection from school by indifferent carers had too often left them adrift and frightened. Valentina opened her eyes. 'What a lovely surprise,' she said but only to herself. Gabriel was insensitive to irony.

'Happy birthday,' he said and then, after a moment's thought, 'Do you realize you are a quarter of a century old today, and in a month's time I will be the same?'

Valentina felt cold and sad. She moved nearer to Gabriel, hoping the warmth of his body would rid her of what her mother had liked to call an 'attack of the shivers'.

'Silver birthdays should be celebrated like silver weddings,' Gabriel said.

'We've been together more or less most of our lives.'

Valentina had meant this to be a humorous response. It sounded flat, almost a complaint. It was, in fact, not at all funny. It was the *more or less* aspect of their togetherness, an ongoing niggle of which she would like to be rid. She thought that she should be sharing her feelings with Gabriel, but something was preventing her. It was not that it would have rocked the boat, because their boat was stable. But, even so, perhaps she was becoming superstitious: tempting providence; not wanting to make changes to something with which there was nothing wrong. She sighed, and their day which seemed momentarily to have come to a halt started up again.

They decided not to go to the nearby park but to one on the other side of town. Neither was sure whether it was because they wanted to be somewhere else – like everyone they knew – or whether they were hoping that a change of location might make them feel as if they were on holiday. Both wondered whether having been more or less abandoned by their absent friends might have brought on a need for some sort of 'Who needs them?' response. Neither of them liked change. They were far more comfortable with the familiar. They reassured themselves that sameness was comfortable and safe.

As they spread out their lunch in the shadow of a tree Valentina looked at the late-summer grass dying for lack of rain. Was their relationship also beginning to look tired? Or was she being fanciful? Why did this Sunday feel different from every other Sunday? Was it because autumn was on the way? It was not that. It was something in the air. Both felt it but could not identify it. Each waited for the other to throw light on the shadows, to work out what was happening to them.

It was true, Valentina thought; they had known one another for ever. It was almost a lifetime since they had held hands on their first day at primary school, waiting for someone to tell them where to hang up their coats, what to do next. Perhaps they were as much in the dark now as they were then, still waiting, still hoping that someone would tell them to come in out of the cold, to take off their coats and make themselves at home.

They had clung to their carers at the school gates, and as soon as they had been prised loose they had clung to one another. Twenty years later they were still clinging. Their need to hold hands, their inability to face life on their own and their fear of making decisions had turned them into Siamese twins joined at the hip in their thoughts. Neither of them questioned their behaviour patterns, neither enquired of one another whether they were content. There were times when they had thought that they were happy, but such episodes were brief and unfulfilling. Each of them thought it was because they had not known what to do when difficulties arose. Neither of them had considered asking themselves why they had been afraid of school all those years ago, why their need for attachment had never left them, nor why neither of them had ever discussed commitment. The possibility that they were still waiting to take delivery of something owed, something left over from childhood, had never occurred to them. They did not wonder why trying to recall past events was suddenly becoming important.

On the way to their picnic they began to talk about times

when they had been happy. They found it hard to recall them.

'I think we were twelve,' Gabriel said. 'It must have been your birthday. We'd gone to the park with your mother because she wouldn't let us play with water pistols in the house. Do you remember?'

'I remember it very well,' replied Valentina. 'You kissed me by the swings. No one had kissed me before. I know it was only a quick peck. I liked it, but I was terribly disturbed. Looking back, I must have thought of it as a major life-changer. I told my mother as soon we got home. I wanted it to last much longer. I wanted you to kiss me again. I pretended it was the last thing I wanted, so I screamed and ran away.'

'It was the water pistol,' said Gabriel. 'I didn't realize its significance at the time. I still think about it sometimes.'

'Strange', said Valentina, 'that neither of us has mentioned it until now. We must have buried it somewhere in our minds.'

Both of them were aware that if the water pistol had marked the beginning of a courtship, it had been one of the longest courtships on record.

'Maybe it was because I ran away when you squirted the water pistol at me,' Valentina suggested. 'You should have run after me, but you didn't.'

'I did run after you.'

'You never caught me.'

There was a silence for a while. Their relationship was free-wheeling into a dimension with which they were unfamiliar. Gabriel sensed a change in Valentina. She was challenging him. It was true that he had run after her all those years ago, but now she was running after him. He found it attractive. What was interesting was that more than twelve years after the event it had become the subject of discussion. At no time before had either of them ever mentioned the incident.

'Probably because I didn't know what to do if I did catch you,' Gabriel continued. 'I don't know whether this is connected, but that time when your mother invited me to dinner, she obviously knew me, but it was as if she was meeting me for the first time. Perhaps she was expecting something from us. Maybe she knew something that we didn't. I felt very unwelcome. We had chicken for dinner. I waited for her to ask me whether I had any preference: breast or leg. I felt it that it was my sexual preferences she was enquiring into. There was nothing for me to be embarrassed about because the portion she gave me was so small I would have had to have been suffering from anorexia to have enjoyed it. My sense of something being withheld was so intense that I never wanted to be invited again. She was using food as a weapon, as if we were in a war zone and I was being starved into submission. Looking back, was your mother coming over as withholding because it was the only kind of mothering she knew?'

Valentina wanted to defend her mother as well as comfort Gabriel. 'You are describing her as a bad mother. Perhaps on that particular day she seemed so. I don't remember her as being quite like that. Maybe having to be a mother again, even if it was only a 'mother-in-law', was the last thing she wanted. She was always at work. We hardly ever saw her. Come to think of it, she did give us the impression that we had fallen on hard times. It was not only food she withheld but pretty well everything. Christmas was a non-event in our house. Other people had a turkey that would last for a week. We had chicken every day, one way or another, including Christmas. I don't think she knew how to cook anything else. Was she saying that every day was like Christmas in our house or that even at Christmas there was not enough to go round? It seemed normal. We never questioned it.'

'At least you had a mother,' Gabriel pointed out. 'Your mother didn't die from tuberculosis when you were three because the doctor said that no one suffered from that condition any longer and hadn't recognized it.' He wondered whether he believed that all mothers were like that and whether he was close to Valentina because she was not a mother. He tried to change the subject. 'My father turned out to be a really good mother, although I expect I must have missed out on something.'

'Do you think', Valentina asked, 'that men *should* be mothering? Aren't they supposed to be fathering? You mother me.'

'I don't think you mother me.'

'Perhaps we don't want to bring out the mother in each other because that's what we've missed out on, and we don't want to experience that again.'

They tidied up the remains of the picnic and stowed it away in the car. On their way to the café nothing more was said. They held hands as they crossed the road but not as confidently as they had years before. Their upbringing was still bothering them.

Valentina looked at the café's china teapot.

'Who's going to be mother?' They looked at one another.

'Funnily enough,' Valentina said, 'it's me.'

BALL GAME

FIONA HAD REALLY liked him. She thought he liked her, too. He had not taken his eyes off her in the pub where they had first met. In the small Welsh town where her company's headquarters was located there were few restaurants. They had both been pub people once but had long since graduated into a world where television chefs were likely to be doing the cooking. Simple food freshly cooked would have pleased them that day, not because they regarded themselves as simple people but because an important business meeting away from the press would have suited them both. She didn't know why she was thinking of him.

Their affair had lasted for a year, and she had neither seen nor spoken to him since it ended. In their year together, everything they had done and everything they had said to one another – from pillow talk to business talk – had been saved in her memory. It should by now have been written over by new liaisons, new interests. There had been nothing since that had enabled her to take her mind off a loss with which she was unable to come to terms. Whenever she felt abandoned and unattractive she played back the meetings with him but had never come any closer to understanding why the affair had ended. She had money but felt impoverished. She had spirit but felt diminished.

She knew that Peter was about ten years older than she, but she had no idea of his actual age. She knew very little about him other than the fact that he might well have been – as he would often claim – the biggest manufacturer of footballs in the world. She did not doubt that he made a great many footballs, but as chief executive of a chain of sports gear stores they were never more than she could handle. He needed her, and she needed him.

'Let's play ball,' he would say. 'I'll kick it to you, and you kick it into the net.' And that is what she did for a year until her firm went unexpectedly into liquidation. He continued to make footballs, but another woman was doing the scoring. It did not help her to see that the new 'midfielder's' features in the business pages of the newspapers were similar to hers. She had been kicked into touch, and he had moved on.

Not only had she been reminded of him because the tabloids were full of his divorce, but he had never told her he was married. She had tried to forget him, but pictures of women he was seen with, all of whom bore a resemblance to her, did not help. What she could not cope with was why he had walked away. She could find no reason for it. They had got on well. He had been attentive and supportive. Sex had been great, despite sporadic worries prompted by the tabloids that suggested he was a serial philanderer and that other women might regard him similarly. She had managed to ignore all that.

She admired him for his achievements and for his business ability. The sporting world admired him because he had bought a premier league football club and two expensive players off the transfer list. She was pleased for him, because his was a success story and she was addicted to success. She could not, however, give up asking herself what had gone wrong. In one catastrophic moment the two components of her life that she most valued – her high-flying position on the board of a major company and the man she loved – had ceased to exist. She was still angry with him, but she loved him. She was angrier still with herself. Life for both of them had been a game, but she had been dropped from the team.

She discussed it with her mother.

'Why can't I let go of him?'

'You never could get over being left. When your father left you were inconsolable.'

'I was only ten.'

'He loved you more than he loved me. He would play with you as soon as he came in. He would give you your supper and read you a story and put you to bed. He seldom let me do it. At weekends he would take you everywhere. He wanted a boy, of course, but you were the next best thing. He took you to football matches every Saturday afternoon. How he could have left you I don't know. You saw him every other weekend, but it was not the same.'

Fiona understood what her mother was saying. She was reminded of a recurrent dream. She was in a boat, rowing upstream with one oar. She thought for a while. How can you make real progress in life with only one parent? There's no balance. With two parents you learn how to be with men and with women. It's been upstream all the way with me. With just one oar you can go only round in circles.

She still had that dream occasionally. Was that what she was doing? She was certainly making no progress. In terms of relationships there had been several opportunities, but none of them had led anywhere.

Had her 'love you and leave you' legacy encouraged her to seek out dissatisfied men, men who were unhappy with what they had, men who were looking for something they had never had? She could not accept that. She and Peter had got on so well. He had tuned into her and she into him. They had so much in common. He was a success, and so was she. Power meant a great deal to them both. He must have known that finding someone as keen on football as she would be difficult. There were plenty of women who *watched* football, but they were a minority. Most of them came to please their partners and were bored stiff. Sport was essentially single-sex. One had Wimbledon, where the girls played with one another and the boys played against one another. To be sure, there were mixed doubles, but it was the centre-court same-sex to-ing and fro-ing that attracted the majority of spectators.

She was sure that Peter liked women, but if her reaction to his departure was anything to go by there must be a great many deeply disappointed women around. He turned his back on a woman every time he found a new one. When he had met her she was definitely 'one of the boys'. Her potency in business matched his.

What if he did not like women at all? What if he used them but did not like them? What if he preferred men and had never recognized it? She had lost her job. She was no longer one of the boys, was no longer a player but merely a spectator. He had moved on and found another boy-girl to play with. But she was strong. She had had a life-enhancing experience. She had got over her father's rejection. She would get over Peter. Soon she would be headhunted. Her confidence, the essence of her being, would be restored. Her childhood would no longer catch her unawares. No goalkeeper would stop her from putting one past him. No boat could go far with only one oar. She knew what she had to do.

BELL, BOOK AND CANDLE

EIGHTEEN-YEAR-OLD Daisy was turning into a beautiful woman. She was tall and slim and her straight black hair reached beyond her shoulders. Appearance had become as important an issue as A levels as she and her classmates prepared themselves for their début on the academic stage. Daisy's friends at the convent envied her looks. Were a girl's brother to admit to his sister that Daisy played a role in his fantasies she would not have been surprised. It was not just her looks. Daisy was admired for her intellect and for the warmth of her personality. She was courteous and kind, and everyone loved her.

None of it made any difference to how she felt about herself, despite the fact that she had been offered a place at Oxford because of her excellent examination results. She considered herself rather plain and ordinary. Contrary to what her mirror suggested, she saw nothing in it that she liked. If others thought her attractive, she thought they must be deluded.

Her mother had taken her to the doctor. He asked her if she was depressed. It was a difficult question to answer. She knew only that she was never happy and told him she felt the same as always. He said that that was not what he had asked her. She said she was not depressed because she did not know what he meant.

'She's not depressed,' said the doctor. 'She'll feel better when she's at university. All her friends will be there. Life will look different.'

But life was not different. It was more of the same. Much was happening that was new and stimulating, but she was as she had always been, withdrawn and flat. She would be more contented if she could fade into the background. But being alone was not an option. Her group lived together, ate together, worked together and went out at night to play together. She thought that the drinking, which accompanied most of their leisure activities, might make her feel better, that alcohol might encourage her to feel that she was part of a happy family. It turned out to be a delusion. The drinking made her feel worse.

She was everyone's dream girl, although she told herself that no one would notice her. Everyone would share her view that she was unattractive, a quiet newcomer who preferred her own company. But she was very noticeable. Some of her fellow students were drawn to the sadness that she could not always conceal and tried to jolly her out of it. Others were embarrassed by her detachment and tried to draw her out of herself. Most were not sure how to approach her and hoped she would approach them. How she looked was not how she thought she looked. Neither she nor anyone else knew why she felt as she did.

Timothy was on the same course. He was quiet and reserved, rather like she was. He seemed also to have opted for privacy, and she allowed herself to like him. He had been to a Catholic boarding-school and she to a convent. She came to believe that they might be seeing something of themselves in each other and felt that they might not only have a common background but share similar anxieties. He accepted her as she was and did not question her about anything that might be personal. She liked that. A wish to keep private that which was private was what they had both been brought up to value.

Timothy told her that he had chosen to read theology because he had grown up in a commercial background and he was anxious to understand more about the spiritual side of life. Daisy had chosen theology because there was an unobtrusive thoughtfulness about the subject that made her think about others as well as herself. She wanted to find out whether religion would help her discover what belief in oneself meant and whether what she had been brought up to accept as the truth could be relied upon. She would have been drawn to any non-intrusive source of information but was particularly pleased with her chosen course.

She thought of theology as scholarship that came to her, rather than she to it. It was the opening hymn of a mass that washed over her as soon as she entered the church, influencing her without her being conscious of it. She thought of the wonder of converting an event, as sad and solemn as a funeral, into a requiem to which opera lovers would pay to listen. It was like an extra layer of clothing in cold weather, something comforting and caring. She wondered why being comforted and cared for by the Church was a priority when in the real world she wished for the opposite.

'I don't think it's the religion,' she said, as she and Timothy walked back together from a lecture. 'It must be something else. If only one felt like that at other times, too. Life's unfair. I've been given something to which I feel I'm not entitled and which I would prefer not to have. If I was not fit and healthy and had not had a good education and parents with substantial expectations I might feel more comfortable with myself. I have too much to live up to.'

Modesty prevented her from mentioning that her looks,

which everyone went on about, might also be something she could well have done without.

'I don't think how we feel has anything to do with the religion,' Timothy said, 'although we have had that drummed into us. It's more to do with how religion looks at us, rather than how we look at it. Perhaps anti-religion attracts us and we are looking for a good reason to give it up. I don't like the threat that lies over you if you don't comply with the rules. On the other hand, I do like order and punctuality. I like the familiarity of the service and the apostolic messages of the sermons. I love continuity, and the Church endorses that. I shouldn't think much has changed for centuries. The rigid nature of it all gives one confidence, adds to a feeling of security. The Church satisfies a need in me I would have difficulty in finding else-where. There is something about the formality that I find comforting, although I may be a bit of a heretic about birth control, homosexuality and women priests.'

Timothy felt daring and grown up as he expressed his liberal views. There were plenty of people who would dis-approve of what he had just said. He wondered whether he might be tempting providence by speaking up for reforms about which he did not feel entirely comfortable. Was he trying to impress Daisy with his worldliness or rambling on because he was trying to cover up something about himself about which he felt badly?

He was around five years old when his mother, who had never previously spoken harshly to him, had, suddenly and very irritably it seemed at the time, told him to 'stop touching it'. He had not known what she meant at first but discovered, much later, that she had a thing about it. Her attitude was presumably based on a long-standing traditional religious disapproval of masturbation that had never left her. The reproof still bothered him, rang constantly in his ears. Would he ever rid himself of time-expired views about moral disorders? Was he studying theology to find answers to questions he was still asking himself? He would have liked to ask Daisy what she thought. Perhaps she would be his confessor and he would feel better about himself. The fact that he hardly knew her might make it easier. Would she want to be his rescuer? He told himself not to be foolish. A girl who he was just getting to know could hardly be expected to help him deal with feelings of guilt induced in him by his mother.

'The idea of an afterlife bothers me,' he said changing the subject. 'It might once have been a reward for good behaviour, but it's being abused. If we were all convinced that we have only one life and that we should make the best of it, we might be less careless about what we do with it. Some seem happy to give up life and opt for martyrdom because a religious leader – who knows no more of the next world, if there is one, than anyone else – has convinced them that life would be more to their taste elsewhere. Wars are fought by religious 'children' who have been promised what no one can ever deliver. They don't know this. Medals for bravery for wartime killing should be banned and awarded only for saving life. People don't need the Bible to find out how to behave towards neighbours and parents or to discover that honesty is an essential social requirement. They learn that by example. I really only like the Church at Easter and Christmas when we all go together.'

'I can't cope with it at all,' said Daisy. 'I can't make up my mind whether I like it or not. I'm sure that it doesn't like me. I feel I'm not welcome. Weddings and funerals freak me out. I sit at the back so that I can leave if people start glaring at me.'

'Why would people glare at you? You must think you behaved badly once and are frightened to go back.'

Daisy thought about this, but nothing came to mind. 'Perhaps it's the church itself. "Not going" does not prevent you from being religious. Church is a place where you are reminded of the presence of God and where you give thanks for what you have received from him. But since God is everywhere it doesn't matter where you speak to him. I'm hoping I'll be better able to have a view on that as time passes.'

Timothy returned to what was on his mind. 'There's something about religion that I do find attractive.' He wondered whether he should tell her of his love of order. He decided not to and said instead, 'I actually *like* going to church with my parents.'

Feeling they had run out of things to talk about, but wanting time to think, they sat on a bench for a moment or two and looked at daffodils struggling with one another to be the first to demonstrate the benefits of the spring sunshine. As they watched nature's silent welcome they both separately yet together had an epiphany immediate in its revelation and for each of them almost divine in its meaning.

Timothy looked at his new friend and saw her not as she thought others saw her but as someone to whom he felt suddenly close. Perhaps he actually had found someone who would help him overturn his mother's unwitting but paralysing effect on his attitude to women and his ever-present sense of guilt.

And as Daisy sat next to him a shaft of sunlight illuminated a childhood memory. She was in church with her family. It must have been Easter, just like now. The daffodils had reminded her. Everything was beautiful. There were flowers everywhere, and the sermon had just started. She thought that the man in the pulpit was about to tell her a story, and she had cried because she was so excited. Her mother had instructed her nanny to take her outside because she was causing a disturbance, and she recalled being pushed in her buggy into the entrance. She could hear the service going on. But it was going on without her.

She had to tell Timothy. He had helped her to remember. She did not know how, but he had.

'You thought your family had turned its back on you by sending you outside,' he said finally. 'Maybe you remember it as if it was the Holy Family rejecting you. The father in the pulpit was about to tell you something interesting and your "holy" mother sent you outside. You've had a sense of not belonging ever since. No wonder you chose theology. You've wanted acceptance by Mother Church ever since.'

One day she would tell him that it was not only that the Church and Holy Communion had been withheld from her but that society had also rejected her. No wonder she felt depressed. She had spent every day feeling that she had been excommunicated. She had chosen theology because she wanted the Holy Book to be open, not shut because someone standing in for God had closed it and blown out her candle.

She was afraid to speak in case the moment went away. Getting up from the bench they clung to one another. Where the daffodils had been she now saw a hundred burning candles. She looked at Timothy. Her light had come back on.

CROWNING GLORY

Promoting an image of carefree contentment, an essential ingredient of a marriage pretending that all was well with it, was something at which Hugo and Deirdre were adept. One ritual they both enjoyed was breakfast in bed on Sundays with the newspapers and reading aloud comments made by restaurant critics to one another. There were other rituals but none to equal the homely image of huddling up in bed. Hugo had discovered a chef having an off day in one of the capital's highly rated establishments, and since it was on their dining-out list was about to comment on it when Deirdre said, 'You're overdoing it.' She had been daydreaming about matters other than restaurants, such as upgrading her wardrobe, and was not quite ready for the newspapers. 'You're working too hard.'

'Yes,' said Hugo, dragging himself away from a requiem for a rapidly deflating soufflé. 'Another year or two and I'll be out of it.' They both knew and were saddened by the fact that the exchange of Sunday-morning trivia was all that remained of the exchange of other intimacies that in its early days had been a feature of their marriage.

Every now and then, in addition to playing Happy Families

on Sunday mornings, both of them felt the need to declare how much they missed one another when separated by business travel. The intensity of this need varied with the extent to which they misused the time spent away from one another with sexual adventures, both real and imagined, which they were convinced would not damage the fabric of their married life.

Deirdre was Hugo's second wife and very much his junior. They had been married for twenty years and enjoyed a lifestyle envied by many of their friends. Entertaining clients from overseas and being entertained by them in turn meant Wimbledon and Ascot, Henley and the Derby. Expense-account dining allowed them the pleasure of controlling the *chef de cuisine* at fashionable restaurants by opting for 'power eating'. Demanding the most expensive dish and then leaving half of it uneaten made them feel that they had reached a level where they could behave exactly as they wished.

There was, however, a fly in the ointment they used to soothe their psyches. Before their marriage, when Deirdre had been working as a stylist in the Mayfair salon frequented by Hugo, their sexual encounters were at their zenith. Deirdre had fallen in love not so much with Hugo but with the sight of his greying curls on the floor of the salon waiting to be swept up by a shampoo child. It gave her a sense of power almost orgasmic in intensity. Women considered hair their crowning glory, and their concern for it was sometimes in inverse proportion to more obvious sexual signals. A sexual reaction to a man's newly cut hair, was, she thought, unusual. Had she realized that men were as concerned about their hair as women, linking it with virility and masculinity, and that what she had been aroused by was a desire to rob Hugo of his potency, the course of their life together might have been different.

Her days as a stylist were long gone. Hugo, his hair now thinner and receding, frequented a barber near his office. He had no complaints about his looks. But there was a problem. Her sexual responses, now that she no longer saw her husband's hair lying at her feet, had ceased. The problem might have been resolved if Hugo had encouraged Deirdre to continue with her career after their marriage. His intention had been to buy her an upmarket salon. She did not want that. A married woman, she had no intention of returning to hairdressing. She was not sure whether other changes in their sex life had gone unnoticed. Hugo was equally unsure whether Deirdre had noticed that he was seldom interested in making love. Both were so preoccupied with other interests that their relationship, once so intertwined, now ran on parallel lines. Socially and in some ways emotionally they continued to be together, but each day drew them further apart sexually.

Hugo lay in his bath, lost in a daydream that had recurred throughout his adult life. A small boy on a quayside was holding on to his nanny with one hand and waving goodbye to his parents with the other. They were leaving for a cruise from which they failed to return. He had never forgotten it and wondered why he had no feelings about an event so clearly tragic. His parents had been killed in a road-traffic accident at their first port of call, and the child's upbringing, while supervised by grandparents, had been left to his nanny. Hugo felt, although he could no longer recall it, that his mother, who had done everything willingly and freely for him, had left him in the hands of a woman who was paid to care for him. When he thought back on it, paying for mothering seemed a greater injustice than their deaths.

One afternoon he tried to explain his situation to his current comforter. It was not something in which Irena was the slightest bit interested, but she tried not to show it. Both of them knew that she was only in it for the money and the odd dinner, but the two of them knew also that the sex only worked if they were fully engaged in their allotted roles.

'It's terrible', Hugo confided, 'being brought up without parents.'

Irena was not sure what was expected of her. She had worked as a garage mechanic in her native Poland and had left her country to earn more money. She thought of Hugo as having come in for a 'full service', at which she considered herself skilled. She was happy in her job but was concerned that if her client wanted her to be his therapist it would not be long before he abandoned her for someone more qualified to fulfil that role.

Hugo, however, was quite satisfied with Irena. He did not need her to be his therapist, but he did expect her to service his needs. He would have liked to have been her only client and from time to time would try to persuade her to give up working for others. The cynicism involved in the query 'What's a nice girl like you doing in a job like this?' escaped him.

He was not quite sure himself what his needs were. Having to pay for love seemed to be not only his fate but a self-fulfilling expectation. Immediate gratification was an essential that was only easy to achieve because he could afford to buy it. He felt gratification to be his birthright and something that should be freely available. He did not like paying for it. Sex was his preferred source of comfort, and being serviced regularly, by one person, was what he believed he needed. Once he had been convinced of his comforter's concern he would move on and put another to the test.

Deirdre was also thinking. She had taken time off to luxuriate in a spa. Hugo never questioned her about her occasional absences, generously considering cosseting no more than her due. Her absences fitted in well with his own arrangements.

It was while Deirdre was having a manicure that a casual remark of the manicurist had panicked her.

'You have lovely hands.'

As if it were yesterday Deirdre recalled the uncle who had

taken her hand and made her do something horrible to him. She was in the garden. She would not allow herself even to think about it now, could remember only how she felt. She hated him for what he had made her do. If she had had a knife she would have attacked him. She had run into the house and told her mother who had hit her for telling lies. All she could remember of her uncle was that he was old and his hair had been curly and grey.

She remembered now why she had been attracted to Hugo as she cut his hair. It was his masculinity, and she was castrating him. Cutting his hair put her on equal terms with him and with all men. Had she been able to do the same to her wicked uncle she might by now have got over what he had done to her. She knew now why she disliked sex. By scape-goating Hugo had she driven him to seek sex with other women? If so, she blamed herself. She had known for some time that he loved her but did not want to make love to her and was certain that it was her fault. She had alienated him through her hatred and her fear of men. What she did not know was that her husband had never given up the search for the nanny who had serviced his needs after the death of his mother. Neither was she aware that he thought he would never find her – but not for want of looking.

That night she got home from the spa, and for the first time in years she held out her hand to Hugo in bed. It was years since she had approached him physically. It was he who had always made the first move. He looked curiously at her. She looked different. A line from a long-forgotten poem his nanny used to read to him at bedtime went round in his head. 'Down in the forest something stirred.' He wondered whether he was also hoping that the next line, 'It was only the cry of a bird', was incorrect. Ever a man of business, it occurred to him that it would at least make commercial sense not to spend money on prostitutes and instead remain faithful to his wife.

CHEQUERED

Sue's sudden recollection of her neighbour, Joan, helping her to pick apples from the tree in her garden twenty years earlier was beginning to bother her. She tried to think what had prompted such an unimportant event to pop up out of her memory bank. The apples had probably not been quite ripe, but she did remember eating them when Joan had commented, for a reason she could no longer recall, that 'things are not always quite what they appear to be'. At the time it seemed nothing more than an off-the-cuff remark. It could have referred to bad apples or rotten apples. If it were about apples it would have been about those that looked ripe but which had been picked too early.

Sue's nephew, Jamie, would be twenty-one tomorrow. She loved him dearly and could not have loved him more had he been her own son rather than her sister's. Good-looking, sociable, always happy – even if he did sometimes seem too good to be true – he would be a great husband for someone one day. Anniversaries often brought to the surface memories that had been hidden for years. She hoped that she was not thinking that Jamie might be a bad apple. That he was not turning out as she would have liked. Anyway, whatever might be going on in his life was none of her business.

At the time of Jamie's birth life had been particularly stressful. She had been trying to have a child, and the diagnosis of her failure to do so was still almost as much of a shock now as it had been then. She was sterile owing to a birth defect about which nothing could be done. Her partner, unable to cope with her persistent concerns about infertility, eventually gave up on her, adding to her distress by leaving her to sort things out without him.

Her sister had also suffered the same fate. Melanie's partner had left a few months earlier for the opposite reason. It was as soon as she told him she was pregnant. Sue wondered, not for the first time, why she and her sister had chosen men who claimed to love them but who then left them when they were most needed. It was only now, years later, that she realized it might have something to do with their father having been killed in a road accident when the two girls were at primary school. Their mother had done her best to bring them up, but it was Jamie they had really to thank for rescuing them – Sue from a lifestyle that was sterile in more ways than one, and Melanie from having to cope with rejection. Jamie's birth had affected her far more than she could have expected. Neither she nor Melanie had been prepared for what life had in store for them.

The two sisters, always close, decided that they would share his upbringing. Having two mothers seemed to suit him. Having one baby between them also suited Sue and Melanie. When Melanie had difficulties with breastfeeding, Sue gave him the bottle. When Melanie went back to work, Sue and Jamie enjoyed each other's company. Jamie gave pleasure to everyone whose lives he touched. He was a beautiful baby. Everyone loved him while he was growing up, and now, twenty-one years later, everyone loved him because he was making a success of his career.

It was Jamie's birthday that prompted Sue's hidden memory. His birth had been premature, and although neither he nor the apples she had picked from the tree that day were ready, both had turned out well, better, in fact, than expected. Her thoughts returned to Joan, who had enquired over the fence the morning of his birth, 'Any news?'

Joan told her later that her enquiry was merely neighbourly, something to say to a young woman whom she would have liked as a friend but whom she did not know very well. She wanted Sue to think of her not only as a good neighbour but also – although she did not mention it – as a possible babysitter for her own baby.

'Jamie was born yesterday,' Sue told her, 'a week early.'

She remembered thinking: When Jamie's grown up he'll not want to think of himself as a yesterday's person. Although it's not funny at all, come to think of it, she told herself. It's inevitable. Everyone becomes a yesterday's person sooner or later. But then Jamie was to be an exception. He would always be ahead of the game. She knew that she was oblivious to any faults in him, putting a good face on him rather than the face that others were beginning to recognize. But, however his face turned out, she knew she would always approve of it.

'Quick off the mark,' Joan said. 'How did it go? Was it an easy birth? Nothing untoward, I hope.'

Asking questions and answering them at the same time was one of Joan's more irritating habits. Sue was not about to waste time discussing Jamie's birth with her neighbour. She was in for a busy few weeks helping Melanie, and she was looking forward to it. She had tried to curtail the conversation with Joan. She remembered every word she had said to her. Having a baby, even though it was her sister's, was an event she would never forget.

Jamie had been an attractive baby. Labour had been precipitate, and within three or four hours of Melanie's first contraction Jamie was raring to go. He was in a hurry from the start.

A contented baby, his birth weight was high – despite having arrived a week early – and his appetite huge. He grew faster than either of his carers thought possible. Everyone loved him. It was as he became older that they discovered there was something about cars that Jamie found mesmerizing. From around the age of six he would watch any television programme in which cars were featured. His two mothers were conscious that in the absence of a male role model boys' toys were a good idea. Jamie told everyone that he wanted to be a racing driver. He was thirteen and at boarding-school before his lifelong interest in motor racing really took off.

They were in the tuck shop one day when his best friend Gideon confided, 'My dad's just bought a new car. My mum doesn't think we need a new one. She says the old one's OK. It's a waste of money, she said.' He looked at Jamie whose views about cars did not extend to buying one but who tried to look interested.

'My dad was a racing driver,' Gideon said, knowing of Jamie's interest in cars, 'but my mother put a stop to it.'

They both recognized that Gideon had told Jamie about the car because he wanted to talk about his father's racing career, something about which he was inordinately proud. 'He was a great driver,' Gideon told Jamie. 'Formula One until he had to give up. He had a few crashes, but I think what my mother really didn't like were the girls.'

'What do you mean? What have girls got to do with it?' Jamie said.

'It's the excitement. It turns them on.' Gideon already considered himself an expert on life in the pits. 'And men, too, probably,' he added after further thought. Despite his size, Jamie's interest in sex was rudimentary. It was not long, however, before his hormones caught up with him and he felt the need for more information. He wondered which of his two mothers he should talk to, and then decided that he could discuss his problems with neither. He envied Gideon his racing-driver father and felt resentful that there had been no man in his life. Whatever he needed to know about women he would have to find out for himself.

His two mothers, who meant more to him than anything, had done everything for him apart from providing him with a male role model. They had let him down. Gideon's father would be his role model. Gideon was happy to talk about him and was pleased that his father was a hero to his friend and delighted that Jamie was taking an interest in him. He might have been less happy had he realized that Jamie's main interest was in his father's sex life. Jamie read everything he could on Grand Prix drivers and soon discovered that everything Gideon had told him about motor racing and women was true. It was not until some time later that the symbolism of the racing driver on the podium, deluging girls with champagne from an exploding bottle, hit home.

There was little that Jamie did not learn about life in the fast lane. The speed at which racing drivers lived and worked not only turned women on sexually but was a potent aphrodisiac to the girls who surrounded each driver like bees round the honey-pot as well as to Jamie. Gideon's embroidered tales of his father's exploits were Jamie's introduction to the possibilities both of racing and of sex.

He could not wait to leave school. He did not want to go to university. His desire to be a racing driver was firmly established, and Gideon's father helped him find an internship in the firm for which he had once raced. Jamie was amazed at how much he enjoyed finding out about his favourite sport. His involvement in what went on in the pits during a race increased by leaps and bounds. He familiarized himself with every car, every engine, every tread on every tyre in the firm's stable in which there were no horses but plenty of horsepower. He soon became a valued member of the team, and the management was impressed with him. Although track opportunities were few and far between, when he finally came to test the performance of an engine his views were respected. Slowly but surely his skills improved, driving him round the track and up the career ladder. He had still to experience the pleasure of spraying female admirers with champagne but sensed that his Grand Prix moment was approaching fast.

He told his girlfriend Anna that what excited him more than anything else was sex and driving racing cars. There was something about Anna that drew him to her. They had known one another for only a few weeks, but he felt entirely at ease with her. There was nothing she would not do to please him. All he wanted from a woman was the warmth of enclosure. He felt safe and secure with Anna's arms around him. He felt equally safe and secure in the more dangerous enclosure of the racetrack. He could not think of a happier combination. His conversations with himself always covered the same ground. What was it that he actually wanted, whether from women or from circuit racing? Although he did not know the answer the question had a familiar ring to it.

Anna might have been able to explain about his needs and expectations, but it would have involved telling her about the other girls in his life. He was worried about the idea of commitment to only one woman. Two women had played an important role in his life. It was not difficult to put two and two together. He could see that having had a fun time with one woman who stayed at home and played with him and being loved by another woman who went to work to support him was hardly a satisfactory rehearsal for the 'one woman, one man' commitment to which most women aspired.

He decided that if that was what was expected of him, in the interests of fidelity, he would move on and play the male role model himself. He had not as yet stood on the podium and demonstrated his maleness. That would have to be the next step. He had some way to go before he could claim that he had arrived.

Every day he was surrounded by 'pit babes'. Like others, he felt his potency emphasized by the obvious willingness of girls to become involved with him. Their presence encouraged anything but fidelity. Jamie felt that he owed it to his mothers to explain that although he might be at risk of promiscuity his path would be straight and narrow. He would make them proud of him. His contribution to his two mothers' expectations of him was improvement in his lap times. There was no point in explaining that he had decided that sex addiction was not for him. He would tell them one day. They would be pleased with him.

The day came, and he discussed his prowess with them over Sunday lunch and took pleasure in explaining the ins and outs of motor racing. It gave him a good feeling. Kissing them goodbye he left to go home. As he climbed into the old banger he had renovated he could hear them talking, no doubt discussing how well their protégé had turned out. He could not hear Sue saying to her sister, 'Jamie is such a lovely boy. I always knew that he would be a success in whatever he chose to do.'

'I agree', Melanie replied. 'But I do wonder why he spends so much of his time going round and round in circles getting nowhere fast.'

SILVER SERVICE

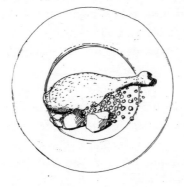

IT WOULD BE hard to find a more dedicated hostess than Eve. Married for fifteen years to Lucas, and with their thirteen-year-old daughter safely settled in an upmarket boarding-school, Eve spent her days dedicating herself to dinner parties and the acquisition of possessions. That she was trying to rewrite an early life that had neither been to her taste nor provided her with the things she believed to be her due had not occurred to her. Her life seemed to be an example of contentment to be envied and, for a thoughtful few, an illustration of the futility of re-enacting unfulfilled childhood needs in the hope that things would turn out differently the second time around.

Eve had drifted through her childhood in the shadow of her parents, both of whom were cosmetic surgeons. They spent their working lives attempting to put a good face on unhappy young women who – usually wrongly – believed that they were ugly. There was little time left for the equally pressing needs of their daughter who was growing up to feel very much out of the loop. As Eve became older she wondered whether their neglect was because they believed no improvement was required or because they thought she was so unattractive that nothing could be done for her.

Her parents' patients had no self-confidence. They were convinced that only surgical realignment of their cheekbones, noses, ears or lips would change them into the people they would like to be. They did not consider that 'feeling unattractive' was a delusional issue that, had it been addressed during their upbringing, might have made her parents' labours redundant. Their wish was that Eve's parents would make them look more attractive. Eve's wish was that her parents would accept her as she was. Neither Eve nor the patients were satisfied with what her parents had done for them. The two surgeons considered that changing faces was a substitute for changing mistaken beliefs. Their disappointed patients shopped around for other surgeons also too easily persuaded to attempt the impossible.

As an adult Eve spent her days looking for the emotional security her parents had denied her. She confused it with the material representations of it. An expensive ring expressing the eternity of love, a necklace symbolizing the embrace of loving arms, an upmarket watch telling her that its donor had time for her, did little to rid her of an ever-present sense of emptiness. In restaurants, even ordering dishes that were more to her taste than her mother's early feeding attempts failed to raise her spirits.

Eve's career as an author was slow to take off. Writing crime novels, in which the protagonists stole security – either by taking valuables belonging to others or by defrauding the illusory securities promoted by the banking system – began to bore her. It was only when she turned to writing 'how to' books aimed at finding shortcuts for women in the kitchen that she discovered her true *métier*.

Lucas was a historian whose life's work, yet to be concluded, was a biography of Prince Albert, Queen Victoria's consort, with whom he identified. Seeing himself as a companion to a wife who must be obeyed suited him. He was considered far-sighted and thoughtful by those who did not know him but thought to be living in another world by those who did. His acquaintances had become accustomed to dragging him out of the past. They were used to his fixed gaze passing over their heads as he contemplated something way behind them or – as some believed – way beyond them. Those who took exception to feeling insufficiently well regarded left his company, and those who accepted having to say everything twice when they addressed him, because it took time for him to realign himself into the here and now, remained his friends. Lucas's life's work, in addition to his role as biographer and consort, was to help his wife fill a vacuum of need gifted to her by her mother on the day she was born.

Although Lucas and Eve were very much at one with one another when their day jobs drew to a close, they were as much in the dark about why the other did what they did as any other couple might be.

Sitting impatiently in one of the few restaurants in which they had actually eaten before, Eve studied the menu for errors and omissions. Not being able to find anything to complain about, she told Lucas to call the maître d' so that she could question him about the day's specials. She asked him to explain the *sauce ravigote* and quizzed him about the *tête de veau*. Finally deciding on the partridge, she needed to vary the accompaniments before she would agree to try it. She sent back the wine they had ordered because it was not what she had expected and was halfway through the partridge before she realized it was pinker than she had expected. When the waiter was summoned she told him very quietly, but all the more menacingly, that he must explain to the chef never – and she repeated never – to serve game as pink ever again.

'I mention it only in the in the interests of health and safety,' she added.

The reprimanded waiter returned to the kitchen to deliver Eve's warning. Eve, now upbeat after having disposed of her mother's feeding inadequacies by scapegoating not only the chef but the waiter, confessed that she thought the restaurant rather good. It was not often that victory over a feeder came her way. It was a moment to savour and definitely one to be repeated. 'I've really enjoyed it,' she told Lucas. 'We must come here again.'

A GOOD SEAT

JANE AND HER friend Amanda sat in the front stalls of the theatre waiting for the curtain to go up. It had been so long since she had been to a play that she had almost forgotten that curtains rarely went up. She had always enjoyed the surprise of seeing the stage set, all of a piece, for the first time. It was Amanda's fiftieth. Jane had asked what she wanted for her birthday, and Amanda said that what she would really like was to go to a matinée. It was simpler than looking for a present, which usually had to be taken back to the shop and exchanged for something else. A matinée had seemed a good idea.

Jane was surprised by how many mothers and small children filled the stalls until she remembered that it was half-term. The mothers looked very young; not much older than her own daughters. She wondered if she missed no longer having small children, but she had done that and was surprised at how relieved she felt. Was it child-caring or childhood to which she had no wish to return? She was not sure. It was not caring for children. That period of her life was over. She had enjoyed it and was looking forward to becoming a grandmother. It had to be childhood.

In the moments before the lights dimmed Jane began suddenly to feel uncomfortable. It was as if she was drowning. It was not the first time that she had had a panic attack, but it was years since the last one. They featured flashbacks to her past. Events she thought she had forgotten surfaced once more: her soldier father being killed by terrorists in Burma when she was six; being sent away to boarding-school when she was eight; and the day, two years later, when she was told not by her mother but by the matron that her mother had remarried. Later her mother told her, although she had not believed her, that because her examinations were pending she had not wanted to worry her. She still disliked her stepfather. What on earth was bringing all that back?

She wanted to go home, as she always did when she was frightened. Now it was too late. She was trapped. Fortunately she was at the end of a row and could leave without disturbing anyone, without drawing attention to herself, without feeling that everyone was looking at her. She felt slightly better. The lights were dimming, and the play was about to begin.

The reviews had been excellent, and she had read the programme notes. She was sure that she would like it. If only she could rid herself of this feeling of unease. Was it because it was a war story? The 1914–18 war was long over. There was no one left to talk about it – the last survivor had recently died aged 110 – but a strange resonance with the battles of long ago remained. It seemed to have affected the collective psyche more than the more recent and equally destructive Second World War. Was it because an entire generation of young men had perished so miserably, so unaware of what was in store for them? Some were not even men, not much more than children; just leaving school and looking for jobs or waiting to go to university and grow up, or doing whatever people did in their gap year nearly a hundred years ago. She could not imagine that any of them would have been planning to go to

France to be murdered by other people's children within an hour or two of their arrival. Perhaps it was patriotism that kept memories of that war alive or the poetry. Patriotism and multi-ethnicity seemed a contradiction now, and if there were any Sassoons or Owens or Elgars or Kiplings during the last war she had not heard of them. She wondered whether the spirit of her grandfather, who had fought in the Great War and survived for the remainder of his life with gas-damaged lungs, might be lurking somewhere in her thoughts, pleased perhaps that she had not forgotten him.

That must be why she was feeling as she did. Her father must have heard stories told by his father. She could not actually remember her father speaking of it, but he seldom spoke to her anyway. She wished he had, but he was always too busy. She had never discovered what he was busy doing, but it was never anything that involved her.

The play added another dimension to how people thought about the Great War. It had to do with trench warfare as seen through the eyes of a horse. The idea of a horse suffering made her unhappy. She was prepared for that, and it was only a play. What she was not prepared for was what it reminded her of, what was so frightening and what, she now realized, had induced the panic.

A horse, which looked and moved uncannily like a real one, was working in a field with a farmer's lad. Jane, who had been brought up on a farm, knew about shire horses, but this one was heavier, more powerful and more magnificent than any she had ever known. She could not think why she felt over-come with sadness. Beginning to weep quietly to herself, she was thankful for the darkness. She had tissues in her bag. They were part of her survival kit. A catastrophizer, she went nowhere without dressings in the event of accidental injury, pills for pain relief and a mobile phone to keep in touch. That morning she had made an effort to leave her bottled water at home. She never queried why this self-reliance was such an essential feature of her life or why others never thought of whether there might be no one around to help in the event of something going wrong. Mesmerized by what was taking place on the stage, she wept when the horse was called into war service, when it was on the field of battle and when it was wounded hauling a gun-carriage into enemy lines. Upright and strong, the horse stood amid shell holes and mud surrounded by dead and wounded bodies and by uprooted trees. There was no vegetation in this field of conflict. Nothing moved. The horse waited patiently for orders, and boys scarcely out of school spent their last moments waiting for other schoolboys to kill them.

Jane continued to cry. Surely the time for weeping had long passed. This was something different. It was the horse. She loved horses and had always had one. Her mother had given her a pony when her father was killed, and later there were other horses. Her mother told her she had a good seat, but it was that first pony who was her friend. She loved his strength, his power, his uprightness and his support, his dependence on her for exercise and feeding and her dependence on him to be there for her, to carry her, to look after her. Much later she realized how far-sighted her mother had been. Although she did not think that she had equated her pony with the loss of a father's support she must at least have seen it as compensation. She wept for a father she could no longer remember, for the horse that reminded her of her childhood. She wiped away the tears that brought relief, finally refuting her mother's oft-repeated dictum that 'big girls don't cry'.

LETHAL

HE WAS ON Death Row. Everyone was on Death Row, but most people had not been given their date. He knew when he would be going. Next Friday, after his favourite breakfast. He'd had hash browns, four eggs sunny side up, crispy bacon and beans three times now. Not everyone felt hungry when their time came. Sometimes the food was thrown away. There was talk of discontinuing 'the prisoner ate a hearty breakfast' routine. He hoped not before his turn came. He looked forward to it. You knew where you were. You got your food request, then they terminated you. He hoped it was too late for a stay of execution. He hated postponing arrangements, although quite a few good last meals had come out of it.

He did not like the idea of being left hanging around while the district attorney talked about him behind his back. They used to say that doctors buried their mistakes but lawyers left theirs hanging in the air. Not the first time he had cheered himself up with gallows humour. He wondered why they still called it that. 'Electric chair' humour would be more appropriate, or 'lethal injection' humour. He tried to work out an updated version of that joke. He should have shared his thoughts about it with the governor or maybe written to the local paper. It might have started a correspondence going. Getting into the papers again would have been good.

He'd have a word with his psychiatrist. He would think of something. He had tried to help by asking him questions about his past. He could not see the point of it, unless he was intending to write a book about him. He had asked about his earliest memories. He said he didn't have any. His memories were painful even if they did recall what happened more than forty years ago. He could hardly bring himself to think of them, never mind speak of them.

There were two memories he tried to forget. The first was the more painful. He was four years old when he pushed open his mother's bedroom door one morning to find her bed empty. He would climb in with her, ready for a cuddle. He knew he was four because it was the day on which his younger brother was born. His mother's hug had been a regular start to his day. It had made him feel good. It was a shock that he had never got over. No one had told him she had had to go away but that she would be back in a day or two. She had gone. That was it. Thinking of it made him want to weep. He had another memory. This one made him angry. It was his father telling him that he'd brought someone home for him to play with.

He had often wondered whether his life would have been different had his mother been there that morning or had his father had not made him feel that he had been pushed out to make room for his brother.

He had once got into trouble over someone taking his place. He had been working in a repair shop, doing his job, keeping to himself. The boss said, 'We've got to let you go.' Just like that. No apology, just 'Get outta here.' He could have said that there was not enough work coming in. A few weeks later another man was taken on to do his job. He was so angry he walked into the repair shop with a spanner and would have killed the boss if someone had not pulled him away. He went to prison for that.

It's bad not to have your rights acknowledged. At least in prison you are treated fairly. There are rules, but everyone usually sticks to them. Like a family. Or like a family should be. They respect one another. Not much bad-mouthing, hardly any violence. Everyone has a job to do. He liked it in jail. Better than outside. He had not been outside for years. The media told you what was going on. Some people, if they ended up in his prison, would give the place a bad name. Going over old stuff was a waste of time. What was done could not be undone. Nevertheless, since he only had a few days to go he might just take a last look at what *they* thought he had done wrong.

So I killed my father and brother. They had it coming. No doubt about that. My brother got in my hair. My father thought he was marvellous and ignored me. He never took me to school on the bus. Always took my brother. It was a good idea to drive into them that morning at the bus stop. Poetry, that was. Shame, though, about the other kids waiting for the bus. Nobody's perfect. I said that to the judge.

One psychiatrist – couldn't have read my notes – asked me why I hadn't killed my mother, too. I explained that I would have done had she not already been dead. I don't know why I grew up so angry. There must be lots of kids that don't bear a grudge after another one comes on the scene. Not my fault. I don't think like the law does. Genes must come into it. Never find out now. My mother got killed during a bank heist after she shot a cashier. Not her fault. He'd tried to pull a fast one on her. She brought it on herself. I begged her to let me come with her that day. I was always faster on the draw. She refused. Too greedy. Justice must be done. Served her right.

NEAR YOU

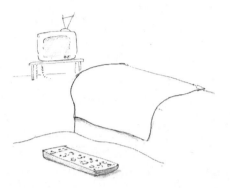

IT WAS LOVE at first sight. He had been waiting all his life for her. Had they already met? Had they been close before? He could not recall where or when. He felt he had known her for ever, in another world, another life. There was something familiar about her. He stared at her. He fixed her in his mind. She might disappear before he could absorb her, before he could experience her oneness with him, before she became him and he became her. Was she one of his circular thoughts? Was she a symptom? Could anyone fall in love as frequently as he? Was she a craving he could not control? He could not go through the withdrawal symptoms again if it did not work out. He could see her clearly. She was looking at him, but she could not see him. He was in his armchair watching television, and she was reading the news.

They could not be closer. They could not be further apart. It did not matter that he was unable to touch her, that he could only see her, that she would be for ever detached, just one more case of unrequited love. She was everything he had expected. What he had wanted since infancy. Seeing but not touching, with her but without her. A recurring vision. He stared at her.

She looked at him. Her look warmed him. He longed for her, wanting her to long for him, to enclose him, wanting to be at one with her.

'Now it's time for the weather.' Without looking at him again she gathered up her papers and extinguished her smile. Night after night he waited for her. He was obsessed with her. Sometimes he thought he might call her. He was afraid of that. He might be found out and be charged with stalking. His love for her consumed him.

He picked up the television remote control. Nothing could be more remote than confronting the real world of long ago. Had he forgotten to take his medication? Why had he not inherited something useful from his distant mother? Why was his only inheritance an unfulfilled need? His craving was not for drugs or alcohol. Falling in love was not bad for his health. It would not kill him. Sometimes it was even enjoyable. He knew he deluded himself. Unrequited love was never enjoyable. Switching off the television, he turned out the lights and climbed the stairs. As usual he would have to rely on his thoughts to comfort him in his lonely bed.

TALION LAW

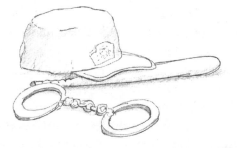

THEY WERE OUTSIDE the supermarket. His brother was in the buggy. 'Hold on to the buggy,' his mother said. 'I'll be back in a moment.' He waited until she disappeared and then let go of his brother and of a great many bottled-up feelings he was unable to identify. He watched his brother, strapped into his buggy in the interests of safety, roll slowly down the gradient of the pavement towards the kerb, towards the traffic, towards his death. He did not shout for help. He did not need help. His brother might have called out, but he was only a few months old and had not yet begun to speak. Anyway, he was probably asleep. A passer-by stopped the buggy, casually handed it back to him and walked off. His mother returned, and they went home. He did not mention the incident. It was no longer of interest.

He was often angry. It was usually with his brother. Occasionally he hit him. Philip never seemed to mind. He liked his brother and became less angry with him as time passed, but he still hit him. Not hard, not enough to really hurt him. One day Philip asked him why he hit him. He had no idea why he hit him. It was because he was there. Philip annoyed him by his very presence. He did not have to do anything.

Sometimes it was his parents. He was always angry with his parents. They were a disappointment. They never did what he asked of them. He found a way of punishing them. They were at the seaside. It was their annual holiday. His parents were sunbathing on the beach. He and his brother were digging in the sand. It was hot, and he wanted an ice cream. They said it was nearly lunchtime; they were going for a walk and would be back soon. Time passed, and they were not back soon. He looked for them but could not find them. He was frightened. It was a long while before he saw them coming out of the beach café. They had kept him waiting. He had felt abandoned. He took his brother and hid behind the huts. They looked everywhere. He saw them asking people. It was now they who were frightened. He was not sorry for them. It made him feel good. It pleased him to think that he had frightened them.

He wondered whether he was really violent. He certainly had flashbacks to events that most people would consider, if not violent, then certainly dangerous. One memory he frequently replayed was of an explosion caused by a gas leak in the flats in which they lived. He must have been about ten. Two people were killed, and others were buried in the rubble. He and Philip and their parents were covered in plaster dust and looked like ghosts. They were taken briefly to the hospital. He was impressed only by the number of fire trucks, ambulances and police cars outside what was left of their building. The flashing lights and sirens excited him. It was like a gangster movie. His parents made a fuss of him. Perhaps that was why he remembered the incident. Perhaps that was why he enjoyed it.

His aunt gave him a tennis racquet for his twelfth birthday. It was a useless present, as he didn't play tennis. He tried playing with the racquet in the garden. At first he hit a ball on to the back wall of the garage and later hit pebbles towards the bottom of the garden. A tennis racquet had little or no play value. Frustrated suddenly, he hit a pebble as hard and as far as he could. The sound of glass shattering became one of the great pleasures of his life. That afternoon he broke every window in one house and destroyed most of a greenhouse in the garden next door to it. His father took his tennis racquet away.

He remembered bullying and playground fights at school and beatings by teachers. Corporal punishment was allowed then. He had difficulty in remembering the details. They were too commonplace. Fighting never bothered him. He enjoyed it. He liked punching and being punched. 'If you hit me I'll punch your lights out,' he would say to other boys. He loved that expression, which might have come from a film he had once seen. He hit people only when they hit him. That was fair.

When he was eighteen he wondered what he was going to do. His friends wanted further education. He did not. He wanted to join the army. He wanted someone to tell him what to do. He could not initiate anything. He knew only about violence and retaliation. If fighting was on offer that's what he would go for. Reasoning did not feature in his thinking. He knew that responding to an impulse could sometimes be dangerous. The army might help him. It might teach him to choose what to do.

He was devastated when he failed the medical. He had a heart murmur. He tried the police force. The police doctor did not notice that his heart was dodgy. He had found his *métier*. When it came to riot control, meaning returned to his life. He was unable to control violence in himself, but he learned how to control it in others. When he hit out with his baton he would reassure his fellow police officers that 'it hurts them more than it hurts us'. 'Punch their lights out!' he'd shout. 'A good beating will do them the world of good.' He sometimes wondered whether that was also what he had been waiting for all his life, not because he thought he deserved it but because it would at least have represented some degree of hands-on attention.

TIMETABLE

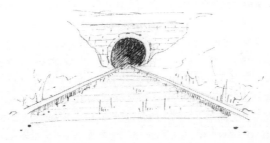

GETTING UP EARLY and going to work, stopping at the pub on the way home, television with his wife after tea, then crashing out, exhausted, ended a day that had more emotional implications than Eddy – the driver of a high-speed turbo-diesel intercity – cared to think about. His job demanded that he knew where he was at any given moment and what he was doing. He would switch his brain to autopilot. This helped him to worry less about the responsibility of transporting a group of people who all had good reasons for wanting to arrive at their destinations quickly and safely from A to B. It also allowed him to detach himself from his passengers' needs, hopes, aspirations, wishes and anything else with which they might be concerned. Switching off from time to time helped him deal better with decision-making and prevented him from becoming stressed.

He was not insensitive to the feelings of others. He certainly loved his wife and his son, but he knew that he coped better with the physical and psychological demands of driving a train if he did not think too much about the trust invested in him by his passengers. All they expected of him was that he carry them without incident to their destination. Their dependence upon him was tangible. But he knew that most of them never gave his concerns a thought. They took him for granted. He felt better able to shoulder his worries, however, if he shut his eyes to them. He did not like to think of journey's end. He was not in a dug-out on the Western Front waiting to be killed by someone who was not reading from the same song sheet as he was. He was just driving a train, unafraid of death but not yet ready for it.

The timetable reassured him. If he departed at a time written in stone he would arrive at a time written in stone. He had always lived by a timetable. It was his instruction manual, his bible. He realized that it merely indicated the train's journey time, but it comforted him to imagine that it also had to do with his own journey time. He believed in absolutes, and the timetable dealt in absolutes. In it he found a time and place for everything. It gave his life meaning, and he did not seek departure from his norm. His bible, like those of other fundamentalists, eschewed variation. It provided him with direction and guidance. It kept him on the straight and narrow, ensured that he remained on the beaten track, neither wandering nor faltering, never going off the rails nor running into the buffers. He was happy with what was. Punctuality, his favourite word, was the key. He knew where he was. Sins neither of commission nor of omission could occur if punctuality was adhered to. The timetable was inflexible in that regard. It allowed for nothing other than exactness. Improvisation and delay were out of the question. Precision was unconditional and adherence to journey time sacred.

Taking care of the train and controlling it pleased him. He shared in the rhythmic certainty of its functioning and felt at one with it. The diesel power driving the wheels was as reassuring as the beating of the heart driving his body. It did not make him feel grandiose but reassured him. He did not seek power for its own sake. It was there. It was his entitlement.

Trains had been a part of his life since boyhood. When

asked what he was going to be when he grew up, he was unaware that a boy's traditional response was 'train driver'. For him his reply was as much part of him as everything else he was born with. 'Why trains?' was a question he was unable to answer. He did not know the answer. He knew only that they were his first love.

Sitting on the pillion of his father's motorbike on his way to school, waiting at the level crossing for the express to hurtle past yards from his face, was a vivid memory of childhood. If they were too late for exposure to the terrifyingly high speed rocketing of the train at the end of his village it was a day wasted. Sometimes he wondered whether his obsession had to do with his love for his father, with the surge of happiness he felt as he waited with him at the level crossing.

It seemed years before he grew up and became a driver of high-speed trains. Time passed, and the unchanging routine of his life, as comforting as his marriage to his childhood sweetheart and as rewarding as the bringing up of Charlie, his only son, continued to fulfil his needs until he found himself considering his retirement. The answer to the enquiry that informed his childhood about what he wanted to be when he grew up was far more certain than the response to the question of what he would do when he retired. Would he lose his power, his health, his strength and his direction when his working life was over? Would he come adrift? Would life as he had known it come to an end? He would have liked Charlie to follow in his footsteps. It would ensure continuity. They would have something to talk about, something they could share. But Charlie had other ideas. He did not want to be a passenger on life's journey or be on a track from which there was no getting off or become a driver imagining he could control his destiny. He had long ago got off the pillion and would make his own way. Trains would not inform his life. He would join the army.

On his retirement Eddy reassured himself that it was only

work he was giving up. Life had not come to an end. He hoped he had years ahead of him and that Charlie might change his mind about the army. He wondered what he might do in his retirement. Already he was missing the impetus that had previously driven him. Something was needed to help him keep going. Sport perhaps? Some of his friends went to a gym to keep fit. Others played golf. Neither of these appealed to him. One morning he awoke with a cough. He was breathless. He felt ill. He went to see his doctor. He had never been ill before. Pills, medicines and advice proved useless. Hospitals became his leitmotiv. Tests and scans followed one upon the other. Experts were called in. His symptoms worsened. Investigations of many kinds and many opinions later, he was told that his heart and his lungs were failing and only a heart/lung transplant could save him. He was dying. On a waiting list for organs, he knew that a heart that exactly matched his body's anti-rejection requirements, and lungs that would fit comfortably into his chest cavity, might not become available in time. He would have to take his turn.

If the power unit in his train had failed, the train would have slowed down and gradually ground to a halt. His power unit was failing. Only a new one would get him back on track. Someone had to die for him to live. He did not want anyone to die, but he had difficulty in controlling his wishes in the long night into which his life was slipping. He allowed himself only to hope that the victim of accidental death, in a road traffic accident perhaps, would have a heart and lungs that matched his own and provide him with the life that he was not as yet ready to give up. He would not be human if he did not occasionally wish for the unimaginable and the unforgivable.

The trauma helicopter brought him the heart and lungs of a young man. The victim was twenty years old and had been returning home from a party on the pillion of a motor cycle. The driver had survived. Eddy thought it an omen, an echo of the life that had effectively begun for him long ago, on a pillion, when he had fallen in love with trains.

The surgery took twelve hours. Eddy lived. He would continue his journey. He felt guilty that he was alive because a young man was dead and tried to reassure himself that everything had been done correctly. There had been no queue-jumping, and he had tried not to wish for someone to die. He had everything to live for. No one could blame him that he wished for life.

His wife and son rejoiced. Charlie had been given compassionate leave. Now he had left with his unit for Afghanistan. Eddy went home to a lifetime on pills. He was surprised to discover that life could be lived without his own heart and without a timetable. He did not go the gym or play golf. He was contented. He spent time with his wife, and when his son came home on leave he spent time with him. Five years after the surgery, five years of being alive when he should have been dead, a senior officer in Charlie's regiment told him that his son had been killed in a road accident in Kabul. An army car had run him over. He had died instantly. He was carrying a donor card and many of his organs had been harvested. Charlie's liver, his pancreas and his eyes went to others who owed their lives to him. 'His heart was healthy,' the officer told him. 'It saved a man with heart disease. I thought you'd like to know that.'

Eddy could not get over Charlie's death. He felt let down by providence, by the timetable and by everything he had lived for. 'It was not time,' he kept telling himself. 'It was too soon.'

Later he was asked by the Ministry of Defence if he would agree to meet the young woman whose life had been saved by his son's liver. She wanted to thank him. They talked neither about trains nor about Charlie, merely exchanged pleasantries. Afterwards Eddy felt better. His son's gift confirmed that there was, after all, life after death. The young woman was alive because Charlie had died. He was alive because another man's son had died. The timetable had not been entirely accurate. It had always assured him that everyone arrived at their destinations, neither early nor late, but on schedule, exactly on time. He was pleased he had retired. He would never have been able to cope with the problems on the line these days.

TICKER

IT WAS APPROACHING Rupert's twenty-first birthday. He was not looking forward to it. His mother said it was a coming of age, a rite of passage, an excuse for a celebration. It made him apprehensive. What was he dreading? Getting old, getting older? What was wrong with getting older? He knew what was wrong with it but did not care to think about it. It was something that he had known for a long time. Something he was trying to talk himself out of. He was afraid of dying, a fear that had been on his mind since the death of his grandfather.

There were still a few weeks to go until his twenty-first, and he tried to keep his fear under control by being too busy to think about it. Time passed with deciding who to invite, who not to invite, whether to have a party or not to have a party, where to go or where not to go, whether to have drinks only or dinner at a restaurant with a DJ and dancing. The need to make a decision took his mind off his anxiety during the day, but at night he lay in bed with thoughts of impending doom robbing him not only of sleep but of the feelings of pleasurable anticipation he knew he was supposed to be experiencing. He was about to be twenty-one. Time to grow out of his fears. Birthdays meant he was growing into them.

He had consulted doctors and therapists. To no avail. They had given him pills to calm him down and pills to cheer him up. He had sessions with a homoeopath and long talks with friends, but his anxiety never left him. He had always considered himself good at working things out. If he knew how his fear had come about it would give him a handle on it, a puzzle to solve. He liked mind games. He could tackle the most difficult Sudoku and *The Times* cryptic crossword. Nothing could be more cryptic than that. The word cryptic fascinated him. He knew he had a problem, but why did the solution remain so elusive? Nothing came to mind. He did not know why he was frightened of dying. Trying to work out what the problem was served only to increase his anxiety.

His persistent preoccupation with death prevented him from enjoying life, from concentrating on his work at school and later at university. He might have obtained a reasonable degree – he knew he was not stupid – but he could concentrate only on thoughts of premature death.

His father suggested he join him in the family firm since it was obvious that life in academia was not for him. It was a high-end Swiss watch business, all of them expensive and sold in outlets throughout the world. The firm had been founded by his grandfather. He loved his grandfather, and while he was growing up they spent a great deal of time together. It was he who had interested him in watches. He was five or six years old when sitting on his grandfather's lap he had been introduced to the wonders of time passing. There was one watch of which he was particularly fond. A pocket watch, a collector's item, complete with watch chain. The case was hinged, and he could see the watch's mechanism. His grandfather explained about the gear train and the mainspring and the balance wheel. The rocking of the tiny cogwheels fascinated him; the rhythm of the tick comforted him. His grandfather, to whom he was very close, told him that time was precious and must never be wasted.

He told him the tick was the heart of the watch and that the watch would keep going until the tick stopped. A watch was the best present anyone could give you. It meant they loved you, that they had time for you. It meant continuity. He knew his grandfather had plenty of time for him, and he always reminded him of it. His grandfather had given him his own pocket watch and said that it would last him a lifetime. When he was eight and was sent away to boarding-school, Rupert entrusted his grandfather's watch to his father.

When his father telephoned the school to say that his grandfather's ticker had stopped, Rupert was not only deeply shocked but was overwhelmed by guilt which reinforced his fear of dying. His grandfather had stated quite clearly that, properly looked after, a watch would keep going for ever. Had he looked after the one his grandfather had given him? Had he let him down? It was only later, when he was summoned to the headmaster's study, that he realized that it was his grandfather who had died, not the 'ticker' for which he had been given responsibility. Almost twenty-one and with his birthday looming he was reminded of the confusion that had overwhelmed him as a small boy and of the mixed messages he had been given for which, all those years ago, he had accepted responsibility.

Persuaded to agree to a club to celebrate his birthday – a rave-up with breakfast at five and then home to bed – he realized suddenly that time, which had always worried him, had inexorably passed; that it was time to grow up. The jury had been out for years and the verdict, which had taken so long to reach him, was unequivocally 'Not guilty'.

APOLOGY

THEIR GUIDE TOOK them on a walking tour of the town. The first stop was a small stone memorial to Jews killed in a pogrom in 1946. It had been erected in 2006; exactly sixty years after the massacre had taken place. She pointed out a synagogue in the distance. Daniel asked how many Jews lived in the town. The guide seemed surprised by his question. 'None,' she said, 'but there used to be forty thousand.' Despite having been born more than forty years after the Second World War was over she was knowledgeable when it came to modern history.

'It's not fair' had been Daniel's response to disappointment as a child. Now thirty-five, he had never been able to shake off how he had felt about being promised something and failing to receive it. The inability of his parents to realize how badly they had let him down. They never said they were sorry. Were he ever to have children he would not be like that. When he agreed to accompany his friend Eli to Poland, where his paintings were being exhibited, he knew that he had to force himself not to back out at the last minute. He did not want to go.

He had never been to Kielce but knew why he was so reluctant. Since he had first read about it years earlier he had been trying not to think of what had happened to the Jews there. That was the ultimate in unfairness. Not because it was the worst atrocity of the war. It was not. But there was something about the unexpectedness of what had happened that made Daniel dread being confronted with it. His nightmare was having to relive the 'not fair' sense of grievance that had dogged his life.

In 1946 a small group of concentration-camp survivors had returned to Kielce after many months in a rehabilitation centre to find their homes occupied by strangers. Not expecting the house owners to return from a death camp, the new inhabitants and their neighbours, believing themselves to be the victims of an injustice, became murderous. Thirty of the returning survivors were killed in the ensuing pogrom. Those responsible for their deaths rationalized what they had done by invoking an ancient blood libel which falsely accused Jews of killing a Christian child and using his blood to make unleavened bread. The fact that the child in this latest version of the libel was alive and well and living with his family on a nearby farm did not change their thinking.

Both the Jewish survivors and the Poles who killed them were victims of Nazi brutality. The irony of one group of victims being killed by another group of victims was a legacy of German anti-Semitism. Another irony was the insistence of some inhabitants of Kielce that Jews had no right to live in Poland in the first place. Expulsion had not worked. Extermination was a second option. Those occupying the homes belonging to the returning Jews had been brainwashed by the distorted thinking of Nazi ideology to play the killing game.

What distressed Daniel most was the expectation of the ex-concentration inmates that something good was about to happen, the promises they would have made to themselves were they to survive, their shock horror at finding their homes occupied by others, the injustice of it all. He wondered how he would react to a town where such terrible unfairness had taken place that had by now become history.

On the day of their departure for Kielce, despite the apprehension that had coloured his thinking for the previous few weeks, Daniel woke up with a feeling of hopeful expectation. The day began early. The drive to the airport was quick – the traffic had not yet begun. Was he hurrying to confront his anxieties and possibly to rid himself of them? He was in no hurry to find out. He was making a journey into his ancestral past, to a place perhaps once inhabited by his forebears, a place where a wrong had been done. He had not known his ancestors but felt as if he was one of them. He would soon be where they had lived, been brought up, gone to school and worked. The day felt strange, but the strangeness was in his head.

The weather was below freezing. He was equipped for the cold, but he was not sure whether he was equipped to confront the horrific events of 1946. A fifteen-year-old girl sitting next to him on the plane told him that she was on a school trip to Auschwitz. Her classmates were laughing and chatting in the rows behind. The Holocaust was on their curriculum. Unfairness and guilt was on his.

At Krakow airport a board held up had Eli's name on it. No one other than Eli looked at it twice. The gallery owner had sent his assistant to show them the sights on the way to Kielce. They had lunch at an inn in a countryside covered in snow. The fried carp brought back memories of things past.

There was a good turn-out to see Eli's work. Daniel noticed that posters advertised future exhibitions showing paintings depicting long-ago Jewish involvement in the area. There was a young Polish woman at the reception. Daniel felt he had met her before. He was in her thoughts. She was in his. He felt he had made an appointment with her years earlier, an appointment to end unfairness. She spoke little English. She looked at Daniel, seeming to recognize him. She spilled champagne on his sleeve. 'I'm so sorry,' she said. 'I'm so very sorry. Please forgive me.' Words he had been waiting to hear all his life.

ASPIRATION

HE WALKED DOWN Main Street on his way to work. It was not the most direct route, but it was the one that took him past the high rise that he thought of as his signature work. He never tired of admiring it and of wishing he could design another building even half as good. He blamed his wife's sudden departure with their four-year-old daughter for the fact that he could not. He was unable to accept that the responsibility for his inability to repeat what had turned out to be the brightest star in his firmament was entirely his.

Ever since Claire had turned her back on him he had found it difficult to cope with the nothingness she had left behind. She had walked out of his life, slamming the door on their marriage, because he had told her about his latest affair. Why she had failed to be supportive and understanding, a shoulder on which to lean, was something he was still unable to comprehend. They had always shared problems, and he could not imagine why this time it should be any different. True, previous difficulties had been financial or family-related, and this one was sexual. It could have made some difference. How was he to know that she would react as she did? He was devastated by how she had taken it and by what she had done. He had not believed for a moment that what he had done was either disloyal or offensive. He had not done it to her. It was just something he did. He loved her. But she had reacted as if she did not love him.

He had thought that they would sit down together and sort it out amicably. It was not so much that her departure left an empty space in his thinking or a disagreeable taste in his mouth; she had left only the taste of nothingness. There was no one to deceive, no one to lie to about where he had been, no one to help him with his lack of discernment. That was the last straw. It was not so much that he had wanted to talk to Claire about his affair but to ask her what she thought about his current girlfriend.

He suffered from a need for gratification into which neither he nor Claire had been able to make any inroads. He knew that he should not blame her for not empathizing with his needs, but he did blame her for leaving him to deal with them on his own. Above all, his feelings of guilt were preventing him from coping with even the most undemanding aspects of his work. His married life, although frequently flat and boring, had ceased to exist, and his enthusiasm, his interest in design and function, his inventiveness, his creativity and his *élan vitale* had disappeared. It was hard to understand. It was obvious that unhappiness and despair left little room for anything else, but he had believed that sooner or later he would get over his loss. He no longer thought this likely. A year had passed since Claire had walked out, and he felt much the same as on the day she left him.

He was convinced that his weekly sessions with the therapist, on which his medical practitioner had insisted, were making him worse. He blamed the therapist, not because she had failed to help him understand why he may have been bored with his marriage and been more or less forced to seek consolation outside it, nor because she offered no quick fix for his problem. She made him feel that the fault lay with Claire, whom he blamed for one thing only: causing him to lose the excitement of deception. He could have embarked upon another affair, but he was too depressed to give women a second thought.

He did not need a psychoanalyst to tell him that the office buildings he had erected were concrete representations of his potency, nor that they should be far more satisfying than the more obvious manifestations of illicit sexual arousal. Extramarital affairs were not for him, she had told him. He did not know why he needed to test out his potency so frequently, but without the energy generated by his conquests he was incapable of designing so much as a cupboard under the stairs. Occasionally he wondered why his affairs had been such a feature of his lifestyle. Did he really need to fight for love? Did he really have to struggle for a woman to love him? Was he replicating an earlier situation with his mother, as the therapist seemed to think? She could have been right. Did it explain why Claire refused to play a role he had bestowed upon her? True, he had turned to other women only when she became a mother after their daughter was born.

Until he got to grips with not needing maternal approval for his achievements – including illicit ones – his inventiveness and design flair would not return. What he found to be the unkindest cut of all was the fact that, while his talent had flourished when he lived life on the edge, it had stifled his creativity while he was living in misery.

It had not occurred to him that he might have been depressed since childhood, but he knew now how depressing the loss of a mother's love could be. Having lived with it all his life he believed that his feelings were normal. It was not sexual activity that had acted as an antidepressant, as his therapist seemed to believe, but the arousal generated by challenging his conscience, the satisfaction of overcoming a woman's reluctance to give him what he craved. Living on the edge was his antidepressant pill. What turned him on was not just the deceit and lies implicit in his fight for love but the risk. Taking a chance made him feel good. His 'win some, lose some' philosophy had sustained him in the past, but he had not taken into account the stake with which he had been playing. For the gambler, the higher the stake the greater the arousal, with life being the highest stake of all. Russian roulette was not his game, although gambling with his marriage came a very close second.

He had regarded himself as imaginative and artistic, before his loss had wiped his slate clean. It was difficult to believe his therapist's insistence that echoes from the remote past were responsible both for his behaviour and for the creativity that arose from it. He could accept that those who were creative might write their life stories. He could also see that sculptors may need to create images of themselves as lovable cupids because their mothers had not made them feel attractive. What could architects be saying? What was his building telling him? What horrible event could have inspired his creation?

He could also see that he might have challenged his conscience in the recent past until enough energy was generated by his conflict with it for him to achieve something worthwhile. He might once have thought that he could get away with behaving badly, but obviously he could not. He had lost that battle. All that had happened was that his conscience had become ever more condemning until it was now destroying him. It was threatening him because he had made it that way. Was it trying to tell him something? He could not get the better of it. At least he had a conscience. That might be reassuring; it was, after all, part of him. He was beginning to understand why it had got to the size it had because he had been giving it a hard time. He knew what he had to do. He would make friends with it. Surely it would leave him alone if he left it alone? The hard time it was giving him was exactly equal and opposite to the hard time he had been giving it. He thought he could get away with murder. In fact, his gamble had generated losses that had wiped him out.

Walking down Main Street he looked again at his building. If that was his autobiography he no longer liked what he saw. It now seemed ugly and overbearing with features that had not struck him before. The top ten storeys were disproportionate. The conscience was taking up too much space and was too big for the overall design. The middle section did not have much going for it, and the basement was dark, dingy and hidden. Why had he not noticed it? It looked fine on paper. It might still look fine to others, but for the first time he could see how much it was like his own psyche. He had read his Freud. He smiled to himself. No more high rises with judgemental top floors. An architect was needed to design a new golf course. It might just suit him. He would start again, this time from the ground up, and if he did find himself in the occasional bunker he would realize that no one other than himself could be blamed for his bad play.

CAT'S EYES

THERE WAS LITTLE, apart from the radio, with which to occupy oneself while driving other than being reflective, playing the cat's eyes at their own game. They were escorting him down the road, guiding him to his destination. He amused himself by thinking that although they might be illuminating the way ahead, showing him the way to go, they were shedding no light at all on what he should be doing when he got there or even where he had been. Of course, he knew where he had been and where he was going. He did not need them to help him with that. He was returning home from a night out with friends. But he would like to think that the cat's eyes knew what he was thinking so that he could share with them his fear of abandoning the straight and narrow, of taking the wrong turning.

He enjoyed being fanciful. He would not mind at all were they to confront him, challenge him with the problems he had to face, demand that he keep his eye on the road or insist that if he promised to do something then he should do it. He would welcome it. He needed all the help he could get to encourage him to abandon wrong-doing and focus on right-doing. If only it were possible.

He would like to think that his imaginary conversation with the cat's eyes was more than a distraction intended to throw the truth out of focus, to assist with something of which he needed to be reminded, something he should be addressing. How many more miles, he asked himself, would he have to travel through the darkness of his thoughts before he could tune into what he would like them to tell him?

He decided to concentrate on the way ahead, not on the right way to go, not on the future, less on trying to sort out irresolvable problems, but more on his journey home. He was fond of the future. He would bring to it nothing more than a past for which he had already done penance. There could be no regrets in such a future, nothing but a more or less clean sheet. He was aware that no sheet could be entirely clean. He was not quite done with what had gone before, but he thought he knew where his problems lay. He would take one last look back. Not easy to do while driving down a busy road. All answers had to lie in the past. But what was the question? If there was a question he had forgotten it. There was only a feeling of unease. He did not need to look back to discover where the past would take him.

The cat's eyes might help. They could see what he could not. Being forward-looking was an asset. One cannot spend one's life looking over one's shoulder. They were better than a satnav. He knew where he was going and how to get there. All he needed was to arrive. They helped him see what he had to do. What lay ahead took place in the dark. He had no idea what the future held. He could neither see it nor imagine it. The past was a different story. That road had been well travelled, and the cat's eyes had given up concerning themselves with it. Everyone needed a direction, but few took time to consider whether the road on which they were would take them where they wanted to go.

The importance of illumination, of seeing things clearly,

could not be minimized. In an aircraft it was a life-saver. In the event of problems the route to the nearest exit would be lit up. While looking ahead could be a life-saver, stepping out blindly could lead to disaster. Careers had to be considered, relationships to be planned. Too many had been put on a road, educated, helped with finding a job and then abandoned. Most people were happy with that. Only a few considered making their own way.

Wandering through life with eyes half shut was the preferred option for most. Some, insisting on independence, opted to sail through a world of which they knew nothing, on their own, often losing their way, their level of need immeasurable, no cat's eyes in the oceans to light their way, no loving hand to hold on the journey.

He wondered why he had become so preoccupied with direction, with where he was going, even with where he had been. Was he thinking of independence – the 'not needing' anyone, which was one of life's options – or of guidance and direction? He knew why these ideas were in his thoughts. It was all about his girlfriend. What to do; where to go. Something was holding up commitment. The cat's eyes were good for keeping him on the straight and narrow but only for taking him in a direction upon which he had already decided. They offered no advice on commitment. Keep on going or turn off the road. They gave him no indication whether his choice of direction was correct. He would have to decide that for himself.

He was pleased that he had worked out why he needed guidance. It was better, he thought, than the guidance he had tried in the past. Therapists pointing him in directions he had no intention of taking. Why then did he consult them? He knew that, too. It was to help him decide. It had to be better than discussing it with his mother, although he knew that she liked to share in his decision-making. His girlfriend was pressurizing him, and his mother was pressurizing him. She always interfered with his love life. She was possessive. He knew but pretended not to know because he liked it. When it came to it, she behaved as if she would prefer him to choose her. When he was young she had taken him to a child-guidance clinic. Was that to guide him or to guide her? Which one of them was delinquent? Was it him or was it her?

He loved her dark eyes, the way she looked at him. She had never remarried after his father had left, nor loved anyone else. She had loved him. She had never left him. It was he who had found someone else. He had never forgiven himself for failing to keep his eyes on the road, for breaking his unspoken promise to his father to love his mother, in sickness and in health, for better or for worse.

IDES

THERE WAS AN unwritten agreement that they would take it in strict turn to operate on private patients who were not referred to a specific surgeon but to the 'centre of excellence' in which they worked. James and Michael had been friends since medical school when, with bravura on the outside but panicking within, squeamish and afraid of the sight of blood, both wondered if they should have chosen careers less stressful, less demanding and more in keeping with their sheltered upbringing. James remembered thinking that if he was keen on anything it would have been dramatic art, rather than the extraordinary and frightening drama that dealt with life and death. The two men had metaphorically held hands on their first day at medical school and continued to do so until they emerged as orthopaedic surgeons never short of work, competing – but pretending not to – for wealth and renown, as experts in the field of sports injury.

As befitted their speciality, both were strongly built. They had excelled at games, the rougher the better. Playing rugby for the university, wrestling for possession in the scrum, the esteem in which they held one another was plain to see.

Although their recreational pushing and shoving could not have been more physical, they knew where to draw the line, allowing one another space in which to develop and in which to grow. Rowing was a shared passion. In the college boat, with James as stroke and Michael at number seven on the bow side, they were in perfect harmony, watched over, dictated to and screamed at by a female cox who supervised their every stroke. They knew what they had to do, but both were secretly pleased that a woman was keeping an eye on how they did it.

Working alongside each other, on their feet for hours in adjoining operating theatres, successful in their chosen path, each had married women who supervised their drive to succeed, helping them manage the harmony within them by the use of moral principles that had never been anything other than sporting. They were still powering their boat, still in tune with one another, as good friends as ever, when, for the first time, Michael pipped a surprised James to the post.

The two surgical teams were discussing departmental issues when a head appeared round the door to say that the England coach was on the phone and that he was looking for a surgeon to carry out a knee replacement. Michael grabbed the call, and James lost the opportunity to boast that he had operated on one of the world's most illustrious footballers. It could have been argued that it was the luck of the draw, or that Michael was nearer to the telephone, or that one knee was much the same as another, but both men knew that such an argument would not hold water. James had not only lost out to Michael, but their sporting principles, as well as their unspoken agreement, had been reneged upon. Was it because it had to do with football, about which Michael was passionate? Was it that he needed the money more urgently than James? Or had he decided to graduate from team spirit to competitive spirit? None of these possibilities seemed likely. James would like to have believed that it was because he had been slower off the mark, but speed was not the issue. Whoever answered the telephone would normally have discussed it with the other, and between them they would have decided whose schedule would more easily accommodate the operation. Despite thinking that taking turns, after all this time, was childish, James felt himself becoming angry. He could hardly be overtly angry with Michael and certainly not in public. It would be difficult to complain about it to him at any time for fear of offending him.

He could not, however, rid himself of the feeling that he had been stabbed in the back. He had often thought about what that would feel like. It would have to be by a friend, a close friend, whom you never would have believed capable of doing such a thing. The celebrated footballer, number one on the world sporting stage, was what it was about. Not the money.

James understood why Michael needed to be figuratively in bed with a star. His wife, who had been the brightest star in his life, had recently left him. He needed to check on his potency and for its power to be acknowledged. He had been humiliated and devastated and no longer wished to share his prima-donna status. Fighting for his emotional life, there was no way he would share the stage with James. James understood how he felt. No footballer's knee could compensate for the loss of a wife, but Michael, no longer top dog in his marriage, needed to be top dog everywhere else.

As always, James and Michael left the meeting together. As they reached the landing James had an unaccountable urge to push his friend down the stairs. Only pity, a powerful defence against cruelty, stayed his hand. He might have lost out on adding another success notch to his scalpel, but what he had gained was more worth while. He had not been stabbed in the back; he had lost neither his friend nor his wife; he had committed no crime for which he could never forgive himself, and – what pleased him most – he had not lost his most valued possession. His compassion remained firmly in place.

THE MILKMAN

Looking back at his childhood, ninety-year-old George realized that it had been his first brush with death. There were others later, but none made anything like the same impression. The death was that of Mrs Connor who lived next door. His mother had always referred to her as 'Poor Mrs Connor' because she had had health problems on and off for years. When she added the prefix 'poor' to anyone her level of concern, always high, would go up a notch. Their names would be added to her list of those on whom she needed to keep an eye. She was like that. It was one of the reasons he loved her. It was also one of the reasons he hated her. She adopted people and was there for them if she thought that life was treating them badly. She was also there for him if he needed her, but she was not always easy to find. She was a 'good' person. No one who knew her could dispute it.

George shared his home with strays and orphans who might technically be living with relatives but who were thought by his mother to need the extra care that a good home could provide. Some of them who had been taken under her wing came to think of his home as 'theirs' and his mother as if she were common property. George wondered where all this extra mothering came from. He thought he must have been poor value as a recipient for her largesse and tried to persuade himself that at least others had benefited from it.

Feeding – or overfeeding – was his mother's way of loving her son. It was intended to ensure that he grew up with five-star lovability. He would more likely have ended up with five-star liver disease had he not been aware that there had always been too much of his mother on his plate. Leaving food uneaten may have been a life-saver, but it was also a bone of contention. His mother did not throw anything away, but she made him feel that she had given it to others more deserving. Sometimes when he could not get into bed because one of her strays was asleep in it he thought that a more appropriate name for her would have been Mother Theresa.

When 'Poor Mrs Connor' was dying, his mother behaved as if she were losing a relative. There had been a fair amount of gloom during the two or three weeks that led up to her death. His parents spoke more quietly than usual. He had always had difficulty tuning in to what they wanted of him. 'You're not listening,' his mother would say. But now it was as if he was living in a world in which things may have been going on around him but from which he was detached. He had heard of the silence of the grave, but Mrs Connor was not in her grave. She was next door in her bed. Everything seemed muffled. If there was such a thing as a palpable hush, he felt that he, his family and his home were enclosed in it. He had not become deaf. His world had become silent.

On the morning when the angel of death was hovering next door, he looked out of his bedroom window and realized why quietness had descended upon them. Straw had been spread across the road so that passing traffic would not disturb Mrs Connor. He was as surprised to see it as he would have been had it been a warm August day and the ground covered in snow. The appearance of the street that morning made such an impression on him that he never forgot it. It was not that he associated it with doom and gloom. On the contrary, he found it strangely exciting. There was something dramatically incongruous about the sight of straw in the middle of a city rather than in the middle of a field. It was almost embarrassingly out of place.

In the 1930s very little motor traffic drove down his street, which led from the main road to nowhere special. Rows of Victorian semis ran along both sides. It was probably less the hiss of tyres and more the sound of the milkman's horse that would have disturbed Mrs Connor. The doctor told everyone that his patient was in a bad state and was not to be disturbed, and his mother told the milkman to 'keep the bottles quiet'.

George often wondered whether his clear memory of straw in the road, which had occurred when he was about ten, was because 'Milkman, Keep Those Bottles Quiet' turned out to be a hit song a few years later and was popular for a while. What gave the title its appeal was probably because being woken up every morning by the milkman was being addressed for the first time. It ceased being a hit as soon as milk was bought in cartons or plastic and bottles were phased out.

It was not just his brush with death and the deathly hush that accompanied it that was memorable, but also the never-ending brush with his mother. There was something about his relationship with her that he had never clearly understood. He did not complain that she did not have time for him; it was more that she often had too much time for him. He felt that despite her intrusion into his thinking she never understood what his views were about anything. Often when she spoke to him he would start singing 'Milkman, keep those bottles quiet'. Was he trying to keep his mother at bay, or trying to drown her out? It did not occur to him that he was directly addressing 'the milkman', whose ever-flowing milk not only almost literally drowned him but still left her with enough for everyone else. He could not have been more direct, despite it not having occurred to him that the milkman was his mother. Had it done so he would have understood why he was forever telling her to keep her bottles quiet. It was not that he was refusing to do whatever it was she was asking of him. It was more that he was giving her a coded message that neither of them understood. It made his mother angry, but he could not stop. That was both the message and his problem.

As an adult, when he was confronted with a serious issue, he would switch into something else, usually related to whatever it was, but humorous and very much less worrying. By then he was able to better understand the meaning of his comments, although their addressees might not. He could see how this might irritate people, especially those concerned with what he seemed to be making light of. He would try to avoid doing it but found it difficult to achieve. As he became older he recognized that gallows humour was his way of dealing with worrying issues. It was not everyone's way. Most people preferred problems to be taken seriously. He was not laughing at them but helping to lighten their problems, to make them less onerous. He did not feel that he was being insulting when his remarks seemed inconsequential but saw them as non-irritating ways of getting his message across. He also thought, although he had told no one, that his ability to make humorous comments was a gift that few possessed and that it was admirable rather than foolish, despite being told by friends that they often found his remarks offensive.

Looking back, he could see that his comments to his mother were clearly hostile. As a child he had discovered a way of being offensive, retaliatory but non-violent towards her, that others may or may not have found amusing. He believed that no one, including his mother, would have been distressed by his comments. He held the key to a secret repertoire of insults that he thought offended no one but gave him much pleasure. Cross-purposes was the name of the game. He remained emotionally and conversationally in touch with his mother but at a level that was anything but straightforward. He was convinced that during his childhood he was interacting with someone he loved and who had his best interests at heart but whose method of addressing his needs was off centre. He sometimes wondered whether it was he or she who had invented this form of communication. His mother was good at best intentions but was brilliant at disguising them.

The debate over his school uniform was one example. In the summer the school dress code was a grey flannel suit with short or long trousers depending on the pupil's age. He had graduated to long trousers. When his original suit needed replacing, his mother told him that since it was only the trousers that he had grown out of she would, in the interests of economy, replace them. That was fine with him. When they turned out, however, to be a different grey from the jacket it induced in him a level of self-consciousness with which he had difficulty coping. He was not sure whether anyone noticed the lack of uniformity, but he did. He spent so much time wondering what others thought about it that his school work suffered. His self-esteem also suffered. He felt no longer all of a piece.

A similar thing happened when he was being kitted out in his Officers Training Corps uniform. The school supplied the uniform, but the parents were required to buy boots. His mother bought him ones with pointed toes because the shop assistant – who had no interest whatsoever in what army officer cadets wore – had said that he had narrow feet. To add to his embarrassment his mother would draw the attention of strangers to the boots while they were in the street. They would politely admire them, despite the discomfort he felt at wearing footwear that would have been more appropriate in a dancing class. The humiliation could take place anywhere. His mother was good at striking up conversations. He did not mind that. He rather admired it. It was when she shared anything that he thought of as personal with strangers that he felt the need to run away from home. It was bad enough having to wear boots with pointed toes – he did his best to give the impression either that they were not really his or that he was breaking them in for someone else – but drawing attention to them was too much. It was an intrusion into his fantasies. His favourite one at the time was that he was a commando in full battledress on a short home leave, having spent months putting down uprisings in remote corners of the empire. He wished he had brought his rifle home when, as they got off the bus, his mother told the conductor that her son was only fourteen. Sometimes she would add that he looked more like twelve. She told a woman she met in the butcher's once that he could have been a boy scout, but had chosen to join the OTC instead.

He realized that she was deflating him when he needed inflating. Why did she do it? While his mother's behaviour was understandable, by the time he understood it, it was too late. She was a carer. The sad, unfortunate and helpless were drawn to her. She was concerned for them. They were her babies. Her son, who had never allowed her to treat him as a baby, wanted to be treated as they were treated. He had always been too self-sufficient. His mother was unaware that she had forced his self-sufficiency upon him by spreading her caring too thinly. She had left it too late. Only when he was poised for take-off had she come round to treating him as a baby. Trying now to turn her increasingly independent son back into the dependent child she had once wanted she realized that she had understood only her own need to be cared for. Her mother had died soon after George was born, and because of the minimal care provided by her exhausted overburdened grandmother she had spent her adult life compensating those in whom she recognized uncared-for aspects of herself. George did not come into that category. He had a mother. That should have been enough. But she could not leave well alone. Enough was never enough. No wonder he used to tell her to keep those bottles quiet. Her ever-flowing breast was not only for all her other babies. His share of it was so much over the top that, although it may not actually have drowned him, the outward manifestations of it and her need to draw attention to her largesse throughout his life overwhelmed and embarrassed him. He was occasionally embarrassed, when he thought about it, by the reply he had made one evening to a waitress at a restaurant the family often frequented. It was shortly after his mother's funeral, and they had decided to eat there to cheer themselves up. 'Where's your mother this evening, dear'? the waitress had said. 'In her grave' was George's reply, in a tone so firmly final but so upbeat that no one present, including George, ever forgot it.

APPETITE

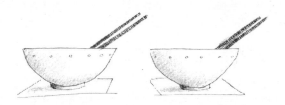

THEY WERE IN a Chinese restaurant. Just the two of them. They were good friends. Their backgrounds were similar. They had grown up together from primary school through boarding-school and army training to fighting alongside one another in Afghanistan. They and their contemporaries marching to the same tune were comforted by the familiarity, discipline, uniformity and sameness that informed their lives and contributed to their feelings of security. They knew where they were with it. Routine was its key, and within it they felt secure. Mealtimes meant no more than any of the other institutionalized events that made up their day. Eating was even more of a non-event, in fact, since any variation on the theme of soup, main course and pudding was rare. They ate not for reasons of gastronomy or hunger or appetite but because it was mealtime.

They would probably have suspected, had they given it a thought, that eating was as much about style and behaviour as it was associated with pleasure or appetite fulfilment. They had been trained more in the niceties of self-control and concern for others than a concern for their taste-buds. What they liked was what they had become used to, the sameness and formality of institutionalized cooking, good table manners, orderly behaviour and boring expectations – anything other than the novelty of eating Cantonese food in a glitzy restaurant in Chinatown that had a curtain of honey-glazed ducks in the window.

Possibly because of the regimented way in which their army eating habits had been shaped they were socially timid and self-effacing in the less structured real world in which they now lived, where they could choose what, when and where they ate. They had been accustomed for years to accept life at face value and to believe that what they were given was what they needed. After they had left the army and gone their separate ways they continued their habit of eating together, always in the same restaurant, unadventurous but routine and safe. They enjoyed their reunions but did not ask themselves why Chinese food had suddenly beckoned nor why, in the past, deviation from familiar themes – had they been contemplated – were invariably turned down.

Neither of them had considered that eating might not always be hunger-dependent but might instead be appetite-encouraging, that taste-buds could become jaded or that the lifting of spirits might play a role in the process. Did they expect that they might suddenly respond to spicy food and the stimulation of the juices that went with it, or did they look forward to a variety of taste experience rather than the mundane flavour of home cooking? Was that why they came? Were such questions to be put to them it was likely that they would struggle to find answers.

Did their choice of table have some significance? Did they prefer to sit in the round because it was more intimate? Did a circle suggest enclosure, or was it less confrontational? Was something no longer inhibiting them and was having a square table between them no longer necessary?

The idea of everything they ordered being served at the same time was at once appealing and something neither of them had been brought up to expect. Waiting, and the delaying of hunger gratification, would more likely have been a feature of their upbringing, and immediate gratification was worth going a long way for. In the rosy light shining from gaudy lanterns hung from the ceiling of Chinese restaurants there was no waiting for appetite fulfilment, no shortage of spice, no 'after you' formality. Hungers were instantly satisfied, contentment not delayed. To share the same food was to sing from the same song sheet. Was it the novelty of sharing a taste, the unexpectedness of the food's appearance, the unusual flavours? Was it appetite arousal?

Would they be asking questions of one another that day? They had been looking for answers for a long time. For the first time since nursery school they held hands as they crossed the road. Formality had been cast aside, a barrier had broken down and sharing was taking place. Next time they might celebrate the discovery of other appetites during the afternoon in a club of which they had heard men speak located somewhere in Soho.

EACH-WAY BET

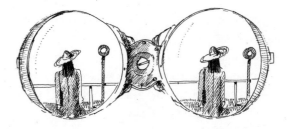

RETIRED PROPERTY MAGNATE Wilfred was fond of racing. His wife, ex-supermodel Antonia, was not. Year after year Royal Ascot was a must for both of them. Wilfred would go to any race meeting because he was addicted to gambling, but Antonia went only to Ascot because she was addicted to admiration. Neither was aware of the reasons that drew both of them to the same yearly event, and friends put their together-ness down to the strength of their relationship.

Theirs was considered an ideal marriage. In households where couples with opposing interests had begun their slow drift towards separation and divorce, well-wishers would urge them to model themselves on Wilfred and Antonia. The reality, however, was that the lives their role models led were separate. Emotionally apart from the beginning, neither had the slightest interest in the other's hopes and aspirations, nor in the way in which they sought to resolve their problems. They had no children, and had they been capable of loving one another it would have consumed the passion each of them needed to reach the heights to which they aspired.

None the less, an apparent attachment to each other was

noted by their friends. It was an attachment that was self-serving. Wilfred needed Antonia because without her he would have had no one to deceive, and Antonia needed Wilfred because no one else would ignore her sufficiently to give credence to her obsession with her appearance and justify her preoccupation with fashion. Both were satisfied with their marriage and with the lifestyle that fulfilled their expectations.

It was unclear to either of them that the needs which had drawn them to one another in the first place were identical. They differed only in the manner in which they dealt with them. They both behaved as if they were owed something, but neither of them knew what it was. As they drifted in and out of the seasonal events that informed their lives, they began to realize that the satisfactions they sought were eluding them. They were hungry for food, for money and for gratification. On the few occasions that they discussed their feelings with each other they agreed that it was probably their mutual urge for acknowledgement that was responsible not only for their obsessions but for their successes. They had been born hungry, and they had remained hungry. Understandably, food played an important role in their lives. They were experts in restaurants, not so much as gourmets but as gourmands. Quantity was more important than quality. Both were overweight.

Wilfred's needs were more demanding than Antonia's. Believing that as an infant he had been cheated out of his rights, he looked to others to compensate him. Greedy in all areas of his life, paying the asking price for anything was not for him. He was unaware that the urge for bargain-hunting and delaying payment in his business transactions was inbred. He considered it a duty to obtain as much as possible for as little as possible.

Having correctly expected accommodation (and full board) to be available to him unconditionally during the early stages of his life, it was understandable that as an adult he would be reluctant to pay the full price for accommodation in hotels. Neither he nor Antonia was ever satisfied with the room provided, and an upgrade was always demanded. Refusal was met with the same angry bewilderment he had shown as a child. Having had to pay for what was his due in childhood by being pleasing to his parents made having to pay for what he thought was his due as an adult difficult. His behaviour was a reflection of what he felt he had missed out on, the right to be provided with a room and full board for nothing – which, if not exactly free, should be at least a reflection of that which he had been cheated out of earlier. The same principle applied when it was his turn to buy the drinks at his golf club. He would be nowhere to be seen. He was particularly opposed to all financial demands made upon him. No one could be more affronted when penalized by traffic wardens. He had paid enough, he told himself. Getting away with it was the name of the game. He had occasionally wondered why he was so mean. It did not occur to him that because his mother had been frugal with her love he was not only taking it out on everyone else but, confusing money with love, he expected the world to understand his need and not make further demands of him.

Antonia was fortunate in that she had been born with good looks and had fallen immediately into the 'bonny baby' category. Admired wherever she went, her single mother did her best to satisfy her little girl's admirers by dressing her as attractively as possible. Although the two of them colluded in their delusional belief that looks were everything, it was not long before Antonia realized that her mother's taste was not hers. Growing up in the school of hard knocks rather than one in which academic distinction was encouraged turned her out into a world that welcomed her eye for fashion. In his search for the perfect woman Wilfred thought he had discovered it in Antonia. She satisfied all his hopes.

It was not only racing which fulfilled their needs. Their winter season was punctuated with cruises in the southern hemisphere. Aboard ship Antonia was admired for her taste in clothes, and Wilfred satisfied his addictive needs in the casino. Neither found the other's addiction of the slightest interest, and each of them took the view that their partner's conduct was of no concern.

Presenting themselves as a 'together' couple, however, was becoming increasingly difficult. The reality was the opposite. Wilfred needed constant input. Life without a struggle seemed meaningless. He was unaware that his need for input arose out of its earlier unavailability. Soon after he was born his mother decided that she would have preferred a daughter and had made that quite clear in her attitude towards her only son. His sensitivity to rejection was equal only to his mother's unwilling-ness to provide rejection. She was responsible for committing him to a lifetime's search for the love which, had she been willing, she could have given him for nothing. He had grown up with the understanding that fulfilment was a matter of chance rather than certainty. Now his preferred source of satisfaction was putting all his hopes on racing certainties and waiting for the arousal he experienced when they paid off. Because they generally failed to do so, his attempts to recreate his upbringing were satisfied. Gambling became a way of life. Horse racing was his favourite pastime, although he was not averse to the casino or the betting shop. The horse's struggle made him happy. Even if it did not win it had tried to do so. That realization made him feel good. If he could not see it run it was not the same. Betting shops were a turn-on but came only second best to the racecourse.

His second preference was sexual conquest. He was not addicted to sex, although he found it perfectly agreeable. It was a woman's acknowledgement of his worth that he needed. Despite what she might actually have thought of him, he needed to persuade her that he was worthy of her love and attention. The more reluctant she was, the greater the challenge; a reversal of a past in which he had never succeeded in convincing his mother that he was worth loving, however persuasive he might have been. He was not interested in sex as sex, because when it was freely available he found it faintly disagreeable. He was addicted only to power, and succeeding when the odds were against him was the ultimate in arousal. This was obvious to those who knew him but less so to himself. Backing a winner was all the more arousing if it was a rank outsider. Confusing power with potency, it was the struggle to succeed that mattered. Anything too easy was of little interest. He was a successful businessman who had reached the top of his tree, and, as he saw it, women found him irresistible.

The negative side of his life was less apparent. He had made one major error. As a young man he had fallen in love with Antonia. She was everything that he believed he needed. She was unavailable, she was an icon and the odds were against her reciprocating his feelings. Her needs were neither satisfied by him nor by any other man. She needed to be admired, but by women. No man could possibly fulfil the need of a clothes horse whose mantra was 'look but don't touch'. In the fashion world, where designers were often gay, she was in her element. No one wanted to touch her until Wilfred added her to his list of challenges. She had never wanted to be on a list. Only to be admired. Looking in the mirror now she saw an ageing icon and a body that was beginning to sag. Although she still liked her appearance she could well understand that she was no longer attractive. Her career was over, and something had happened that neither she nor he had difficulty in under-standing. It had come upon them gradually. Like Antonia, Wilfred seemed to be ageing. His ambitions began to flag. He had made many conquests and had backed many horses, but they ceased to have the desired effect. He had given up business some time ago and believed that it would provide him with more time for leisure pursuits. What were they? Did he have other interests, and if so where had they gone? He would retire from business. He felt pleased with his decision.

Wilfred and Antonia looked at one another. They saw each other as if for the first time. No longer rivals, they had given up looking for what had been lost for ever. They had each other. She looks nice, he thought. Antonia thought that she rather liked him. It had taken them a long time to discover what they had spent a lifetime denying they needed.

JAM ON IT

DANIEL WAS EMBARRASSED. He'd done it again. He thought he'd been funny, but it was just another barbed innuendo. All it did was take its recipient down a peg or two. He was not aware that it was what he had intended, but he had to stop doing it. His friends no longer thought of him as amusing. More likely offensive, if the truth was known. Even his friend William had been hurt by a remark he had made that morning. Not having seen one another for a while they had met for a drink, and within a few moments he had succeeded in making William angry.

They had been discussing William's impending marriage. This would have been the moment to congratulate him on his good fortune, to wish him well, to express his readiness to share in his happiness and to tell him that he was up for anything he might want any help with. Instead, Daniel was unable to prevent himself from making a comment that even he could now see was not only facetious but offensive. He remembered what he had said and could see that it was hurtful, but he had not intended to offend him. It had to do with William's prospective bride's supposedly prosperous background. He had said something like, 'You won't have to do a day's work from now on then, ha-ha.' William took it to mean that Daniel thought he was marrying for money. Since what he was doing was just that, it made him angry.

Daniel tried to reassure himself that William was over-sensitive and could not take a joke. But since he knew that there was some truth in his remark it would have been all the more reason for keeping such comments to himself. He had always been good at the one-liner. They made people laugh, although William had told him more than once that innuendo might be amusing but was invariably hostile. Why would he want to hurt his friend? Where did it come from? Had he been brought up to be a smartass, to be amusing or, more likely, cutting? His mother had told him that he had been a com-placent and easy-to-manage baby from the moment he was born. There were no clues there. He admired her ability to recall virtually every feature of his infancy. He wondered whether she had any inkling as to how he might turn out while she waited for him to make his much delayed appearance on the scene more than forty years earlier. Daniel had been on the shortlist of names his parents had planned. Later they tacked 'dreamy' on to it. As soon as activity or passivity as a behavioural option kicked in, there had been no doubt about his preference. Compliance was the name of his game. He was a 'good' baby from the word go. He did not rock any boats. So from where did the waspish-ness come?

It was only much later that Daniel realized that although 'good' babies might be a major source of satisfaction to parents by not making their presence felt as infants, they became prone to behavioural problems when they were adults.

He could not have known that had he been more demanding as a baby he would have received sufficient input to provide him with enough contentment to last a lifetime. Was that why he was so demanding as an adult? Had it encouraged him to envy what others had, simply because he had not been given it? If it was contentment out of which he had been cheated, why did he ridicule others with his jokes, rob them of their sense of fulfilment, irritate everyone by being dismissive of their opinions? He was an expert on put-downs. Having grown up feeling unworthy of attention, his banter robbed others of their sense of self-worth. He had certainly succeeded in robbing William of whatever joy he may have been experiencing about his forthcoming marriage.

Being undemanding might have made his parents happy. It had not made him happy. Provoking responses provided him with some of the input on which he had missed out, but it did nothing to raise his level of contentment.

'He looks as if he's sleeping, so I won't disturb him,' his mother told him she used to say when her friends came to visit and presumably to admire him. 'Creep in and have a quick look. He's lovely, isn't he?' He presumed no one would have been likely to disagree, at least to her face, with his mother's evaluation of him. He was a 'good' baby. Had he been a 'bad' baby in constant need of attention, feeding, changing, acknowledging or just passing the time of day in cuddles and babble talk with his mother he might now have been less in need of input and constant attention, less hostile (disguised as humour) towards those whose contentment he envied.

He blamed his father for encouraging his mother in her neglect of him with comments such as 'Let sleeping dogs lie' whenever she was tempted to pick him up and play with him. He concluded that men as well as women disliked him and converted their animosity into a self-fulfilling prophecy by offending them.

His mother seemed never to have got over how fortunate she had been in having produced her paragon. He had never woken her in the night or disputed her feeding schedule and would lie contentedly all day in his pram looking up at the trees in the garden.

If the amount of lifetime compliance was the same for most people, he must have used up almost all of his allocation very early. When he was about ten, he switched from flexibility to inflexibility and replaced compliance with intransigence. The placid baby about whom his mother never tired of talking and about whom he had become tired of hearing was growing into the man referred to by those who knew him as difficult.

Eager to disprove his mother's views about how he felt about his world (and hers), Daniel was cold and disobliging throughout his adolescence. Although never actively hostile, before he would consider acting upon any request his mother might make of him he would insist upon a full explanation of the reasons which lay behind it. Had his mother been sensitive to his needs she might have asked herself why he was so provocative, why he never accepted what was, why he questioned everything and invariably wanted more, be it information, gratification or food. Although her attitude towards him might have increased his fund of knowledge, it succeeded only in making him both demanding and overweight.

It was not only his mother who found relating to him difficult. His behaviour provoked outbursts of irritation in nearly everyone who knew him. He evolved from being a 'good' baby into an irritating adult who would insist on maximum input from his environment, particularly when it was not readily available.

While he was at school it was a minor problem, but it became a major one when he decided to make the army his career. The unspoken 'do or die' ethos of the battlefield – unchanged since the Crimea – had no bearing whatsoever on his time in the cookhouse. He knew why he had been put there and saw no reason to question it. As soon as warfare beckoned, however, his insistence on 'needing to know' ensured that he and the army realized that they were unsuited to one another. Leaving as soon as his contract expired he decided that he would try to work out the reasons for his unpopularity.

He was in his early twenties before he – who relied on his hostile psyche as others relied on their physique to confront the slings and arrows to which they were exposed – decided to examine his inner self. While his friends were attending gyms or jogging in the park to improve their physiques, Daniel would be in bed exercising his psyche by trying to generate concerned interest in whoever was prepared to assist him in that task.

'You know, I haven't been loved enough.'

Marina, his long-term partner, who was barely awake from a night of insufficient sleep, in a state of post-coital exhaustion and not in any condition to agree or disagree with what he had said, thought briefly that she might feel the same way but saw little point in explaining that to Daniel. She was also hungry for food and decided to get up and look for something to eat instead.

Trying to resist humming Patsy Cline's 'Hunger for Love' lyrics and wondering why a fifty-year-old pop ballad had suddenly come to mind she realized that she and Daniel might have a lot more in common than she thought.

'Toast?' she asked, pulling on her robe.

He nodded. 'Don't forget the marmalade.' It was not intended as a rebuke and she did not take it as one.

She smiled. 'You always did want jam on it.'

Daniel stopped dead in his tracks. No one had ever said that to him before. He had barely acknowledged it himself.

Had he at last found a woman, although she may have been unaware of it, who not only punched at his weight but actually understood his problem? Briefly reflecting that his mother had never put jam or anything else on it, he got out of bed to help Marina make the coffee.

FULLY BOOKED

N O ONE ENJOYED the monthly meetings of the dining club more than Jeremy. Always smartly dressed, never at a loss for words and thought to be leading a hectic life, he remained regularly in touch with the half-a-dozen or so other consultants whose retirement date had more or less corresponded with his own. It was ten years since they had agreed to meet on a regular basis. Having worked as a team in the same department at their teaching hospital they had decided that their meeting place would be in the domed atrium of the Royal Society of Medicine, of which they were retired Fellows. There were comfortable chairs and a bar where they would assemble at the appointed time.

Although they described themselves essentially as a 'dining club', in the early days of their retirement they had also been involved in other activities. There were academic meetings and the occasional concert at the college, former colleagues with whom to pass the time of day and, of course, the library. All this sounded good, but they had come to feel that what was on offer was like a restaurant where the menu might read well but where the food fell short of its description. They missed their patients.

As time passed, distancing them ever further from working lives which over the years had come between them and their families and many social activities, they found themselves becoming ever more disenchanted with academia. They now looked forward not to clinical meetings but to sharing reminiscences, eating, drinking then disappearing into the darkness from which they had come. They thought of it as darkness because, although it might still be light, none of them had any idea about where the others lived, about their families or much else about them other than how they presented at their monthly meetings. All they knew with certainty was that they were paediatricians whose expertise had lain in several sub-areas of their speciality, including radiology, neurology, surgery, psychiatry and dentistry. Their working lives had been spent with sick children, dependent upon them if not because of illness then because of age-related reasons. None of them were capable of adult conversation. They had not remarked this while they were working, but once they had retired they noticed that they had very little to say for themselves. Whether they had chosen to spend their lives with children because that was a level of social interaction with which they were comfortable, or whether, over time, they had taken on the colouring of their surroundings, they did not know. If asked they would almost certainly have opted for the latter explanation. The exception was Nicholas, a paediatric dentist who was at least fluent in non-transactional babble conversation.

Jeremy, a psychiatrist, had for some time formed a view about which option was the more likely. Since no one asked him he decided to keep his opinion to himself. The group's conversational skills reminded him of a psychoanalyst's Christmas party he had once attended. Psychoanalysts, who spent their working lives waiting for their patients to speak to them, were gathered together in small groups clutching their glasses and waiting in silence for someone to say something. It made for the most tedious gathering he had ever attended. He had found the party interesting none the less and wondered why this was. It would come to mind frequently. Something would remind him of it. It was puzzling, except perhaps to a psychoanalyst who might not think of it as anything other than normal.

Jeremy was convinced that, among his friends, it also had to do with a fear of being unable to make a contribution, a fear of being thought foolish, a fear of revelation. He noticed that none of them said very much about themselves. Could it really be that they had spent so long in the company of children that they had lost the ability to have informed discussions about anything, or did they have something to hide? Gossip was all very well. No effort was required. They could relax and ramble on. Was that it, he wondered? He missed the children, not because they had had challenging health problems that required the team's considerable expertise to resolve before reuniting them with their worried families but because they were children. He loved them for their innocence, for their trust in the doctors and nurses who looked after them, for the joy they gave to those who cared for them and for the waves of gratitude that emanated from them when they got better. Often one of the others would also remember a child that had given him so much happiness, given so much substance to his life.

Most of the group had their own families and were caring and loving parents themselves. But the love Jeremy had for the children was not a duty, was not a result of parental responsibility. It was purer than that. It was a love more genuine because it was not a duty. It was a choice. His young patients were his life. Often he thought that if it were not for the dining club there would now be little to live for in his retirement. Much of his life consisted of memories. He loved his memories. They were a comfort to him.

When monthly meetings came to an end diaries were consulted to find a suitable date for the next meeting. Days and dates were bandied about. All of them seemed so busy. Nicholas thought Jeremy the busiest. Looking over his shoulder he once took a quick peek at his diary. He never did it again. Every page was blank.

MAMA MIA

THEY WERE A happy couple. They had married when Joan was twenty-four and William was twenty-six. They could not have been more loving, more attentive, more concerned for one another. From the moment they met William knew he had found the woman for whom all his life he had been waiting. His marriage provided him with a feeling of contentment that he had never before experienced. The idea of Joan being by his side for ever filled him with joy.

But there was something that worried him. From time to time her job would take her three thousand miles away to her firm's New York office for a few days. He would mourn her absence and experience it as a loss so intense that it was almost as though she had died. He could not live without her. He would lie in bed at night unable to sleep, fantasizing that something terrible had happened and fearing that she would never come back. His joy when she did return was so over-whelmingly inappropriate and powerful that he felt he had to protect her from it.

He was used to separation. He had been sent away to school when he was seven. He did not remember being frightened then and accepted being parted from his parents as normal. They visited him every term on sports day and he felt all right when they left. He was not sad then, did not think they were going to die and was usually pleased for them to leave because his mother had a tendency to treat him as a baby in front of his friends. It was much later that he wondered why, if she did think of him as a baby, she had not kept him at home for longer instead of sending him to boarding-school and embarrassing him. Although he resented being parted from his home he never felt as he did when Jane left him for two days. Some of the boys probably did miss their parents, particularly at the beginning of term, but the matron always sorted them out. That was her job.

When he was about ten he discovered that *mater* was Latin for mother and that her job was to stand in for his mother should it become necessary. He decided that he would cope with whatever bothered him on his own. He could not imagine that a mother with eight hundred children would be able to spend much time with any of them. By the time she had got round to him he would most likely have got over whatever it was that was bothering him. His sister had told him that at her school the matron was referred to as Mother Superior, and what she was puzzled by was how someone who was not her mother could possibly be thought of as being superior to her actual mother.

Such anomalies were for children to sort out, not married adults. He would put his anxiety about Joan's absences out of his mind and would try not to think about it. When she went away again he would cope as he had when he was at boarding-school, although then it was he who had gone away while the person who loved him remained at home. It had not worried him then. Nothing had worried him since then, apart from his recurring dream.

For as long as he could remember he had had a dream in

which he was lost and unable to find his way home. His surroundings would become increasingly unfamiliar until eventually he had no idea where he was. He would wait at bus stops for buses that never came. He would look for taxis that had ceased to exist. He would ask passers-by to point him in the right direction, but no one knew where that was. Sometimes they thought they did know but pointed out ways he could never take because hostile landscapes, rough seas or high mountains would lie between him and where he needed to be. There would be no transport to take him across what was blocking his way to where he would be safe. Where he needed to go seemed to drift ever further away, although always remaining just visible in the distance. Being cut adrift was one theme of his dream; another was that no one seemed to understand what he needed. He concluded that his wish to be in a safe environment was to be for ever thwarted because there were so many obstacles obstructing it. He would invariably wake up in a sweat, wondering who it was who had placed the obstacles between him and his home and thankful that he was safe. He would forget about his dream until he had it again. It was always a variation on the same theme. He was lost and unable to get home.

His earliest memory was when he was almost five and was being taken by his nanny to his primary school. It was his first day and he had clung to her like a limpet. He wanted her to take him home. He lost that battle. He was prised loose and handed over. Later his mother had told him what a brave boy he had been. He was a brave boy. Never again did he reveal his feelings. He erased insecurity, need, attachment and mothering from his thinking. He had survived boarding-school but he was unable to survive being separated from his wife.

'I'm glad you're back,' he said.

'So am I. I've got some good news.'

He waited to hear what it was. Had she been given a bonus? A promotion, perhaps. She smiled at him.

'Can't you guess?' she said. 'I'm going to have a baby. Good, isn't it?'

He hugged her. No more going away. No more anxiety about separation. No more dreams of being cast aside. When the baby came she would be at home. They would be a family. He was not familiar with family life, but it was not too late to learn.

Joan's pregnancy was the happiest time in his life. Their levels of concern for one another had never been higher. He was by her side when she welcomed Nicky into the world and by her side when she fed him. William, Joan and the baby talked to one another from the beginning. They understood one another and were at one. Then something happened that neither he nor Joan understood. Despite his love for his wife and his need for her, when sexual activity resumed he was unable to make love to her. It was not that he no longer found her attractive, nor that Joan's procreative needs were satisfied and that she was now turning away from him. It was that the idea of sex with his baby's mother had become distasteful. Sex with Joan had hitherto been fine. Sex with Nicky's mother was not.

Nicky's mother was not his mother, he told himself. He hardly knew his mother. When he needed mothering he supposed that she must have been around, but he knew it not to be true. He remembered the struggle at the school gates. He had wanted to go home but had never made it. At the time he had conceded defeat, but he had dreamed about his mother's inaccessibility ever since. He had been cheated out of motherly love when he needed it most.

He realized that the first time he had felt really happy, comfortable and at home was when he married Joan. Their home was a haven. Nicky's birth was a new beginning not only for Nicky but for him. But it was not for him; it was for Nicky. Nicky talked to Joan and Joan talked to Nicky. Their conversation had begun. His conversation with his mother had only started when he went to school, but even then she had not been listening. Had he been trying to tell her that she still owed him something which no nanny or matron could ever provide?

Joan was not his mother. She was Nicky's mother. It was Nicky's mothering needs she was addressing, not his. How easy it had been to slip into role confusion. Sex with Nicky's mother was OK. Sex with his own mother was not.

TIME WARP

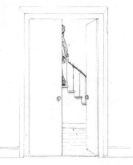

Despite the intensity of their love for one another Keith and Miranda feared committing themselves formally. Preferring an open-ended relationship to one in which they were convinced they would feel trapped, they had never married. Their intention was to remain as one for ever, not because of any formal obligation but because they loved one another, an attachment stronger, or so they believed, than the marriage bond. Always close, they had become even closer after Miranda became pregnant.

They had no concerns about their agreement to cohabit rather than marry other than when the occasional disagreement made them conscious of how easy it would be for one or other of them to walk away. No lawyers, no maintenance decisions, just goodbye. Their fear of abandonment, however, was even greater than their fear of commitment and served only to strengthen their bond. Both were aware of their tendency to cling, but since they regarded it as comforting, rather than a reflection of immature dependent needs, they chose to ignore it.

They knew that something from the past must have led to

their commitment phobia, which they had come to think of as something they shared, a possession that would never trouble them because neither had the slightest wish to be rid of it. They were joint owners and believed, although it seemed paradoxical, that it strengthened rather than weakened the bond between them.

On days when issues arose on which they were unable to agree they were more open to reflecting on events in their upbringing which might have been responsible for their phobia. After all, they told one another, if their mothers' earliest embraces had failed to comfort them, later embraces might trigger these memories and would also fail. But they were certain that they would be able to deal with this and simply ignored it. They also ignored the probability that if their dependent needs had not been dealt with when it had been the time to do so; they might still be looking for someone – or something – to satisfy this need, now clearly time-expired. Since they considered themselves grown up and completely independent, this would be another concern that need never bother them.

Both were adults, intellectually stable and comfortable with their past. Neither of them could believe that their commitment phobia could have arisen as a consequence of thoughtless parenting. Many evenings were spent discussing and debating issues that their friends might be dealing with but that they would not have to face. What bothered others would never bother them. They had explored marital difficulties in their reading and believed that in the unlikely event of problems arising they would resolve them. They would know what to look out for. It was obvious to those who knew them that the problem they had failed to resolve was not their fear of being trapped in a situation from which they were unable to escape but of being in a situation in which their needs were in the control of others. It was no coincidence that neither Keith nor Miranda would go on the London Underground network, enter a lift, travel by plane, sit in the middle of a row in a theatre or even sit in the back of a two-door car. They avoided any enclosure from which escape might prove difficult. They had not realized that avoiding a feared situation rather than confronting it was more likely to result in its perpetuation than its resolution. They colluded in the mistaken belief that since both of them suffered from the problem it ceased to be one. It was not long, however, before they discovered this premise to be faulty.

Miranda's father was a businessman who worked all hours, was here, there and everywhere, kept to no domestic timetable and caused her orderly, obsessionally tidy mother immense frustration. When Miranda was a baby her mother, who had qualified in medicine before she married, discovered some relief from her obsessionality by switching from working as a GP to training as a psychotherapist. She was happy in an environment where she could practise role reversal. Dealing with her problem in someone else for an hour was strangely comforting. She could not wait to get back to work after Miranda's birth. She loved her baby, but like all infants Miranda was messy, unpredictable and time-disruptive. Miranda's recollections told her that her mother was always around to lend an ear to her problems for which her father never had time. As time passed she realized that lending an ear more and more to the problems of patients seemed to prevent her mother from finding time to attend to the problems of her daughter.

Looking back she could see that her mother had not deliberately neglected her but that she was merely shifting her increasingly independent daughter from first place in her attentions to the second place previously occupied by her patients. Miranda was reminded of this when she debated an issue with Keith.

What she noticed was that when a topic became heated

Keith would not become physically unavailable to her as her mother had been but would turn his head away and become engrossed in other things. He did that while she was discussing money matters and pointing out the effect that inflation was having on the housekeeping budget. It was not a very interesting topic but an essential one.

'What are you staring at, Keith?'

'Nothing. I'll be back in a moment. I've got to Google something.' He left the room.

He was entitled to look out of the window or glance at the newspaper that lay next to him on the sofa, but Miranda wished that he would pay more attention to her. Perhaps he had not heard what she had said.

'The supermarket bills have gone up.' She raised her voice in case he had not heard. There was a fair amount of traffic going by.

It was clear to Miranda that Keith could hear what she was saying. Turning up the volume had caused him to switch from looking away to going away. She tried to work out why that was but had no idea. She realized that Keith was phobic about more than just not wanting to marry her. He did not want to do anything about which she felt passionate. Was insistence, like speaking more loudly, anything to do with commitment? Only as a child, she thought. As a child you are trapped. You have to do as you are told. As an adult you can walk away. Was that what Keith had done?

She registered a shift in the 'never a problem that could not be sorted out' aspect of their relationship but could not work out what it was.

Changes were taking place. She wondered what had happened to their resolve to talk things through, to work things out. Body language was taking over. Keith was thinking with his feet. She wished she could have shared her thoughts with him, but his feet had removed him from discussion.

Keith was at his computer. Upstairs, out of range of Miranda's reproof, he, too, was concerned that something had slipped out of focus in their relationship. He had gone from thinking out to walking out. Miranda had changed, he told himself. Perhaps it was because she was pregnant. He wondered whether he had also changed. Could the prospect of a baby be having an effect on him?

What was he supposed to do? What had they agreed on? He knew that he should be reflecting on something from the past that might have contributed to a 'walking away' rather than a 'staying put' contemplation of the problem. Both had convinced themselves that talking things through would inevitably be followed by resolution.

He thought of his childhood. His mother had figured mainly in it. In fact, no one else had figured in it at all. He was everything to his mother. She was everything to him. She had often told him that, and he had never been allowed to forget it. He had had only one parent for as long as he could remember. His father had abandoned them both soon after his son was born. The only good side to that perhaps was that he had less to take into account, less to be influenced by; although even the absence of something can be influential, he reminded himself. His upbringing was very much one note; a shrill note, now that he came to think of it. His mother was very demanding; demanding and loving at the same time. Not a good combination. It was hard to refuse someone who says she loves you. He felt suddenly cold. Miranda was not his mother. But she had asked him for something, and he had walked away. He did not even want to consider that as something to refute. That would be awful. He could not possibly go through all that again.

Something was nagging him. She was going to be a mother. Only a few months to go and the parent–child cycle would start all over again. Could he stand it? Should he walk away from it as his father had? Maybe his father had had the same problem? He seldom thought of him at all. He had known little about him because his mother had never spoken about him. He was angry with her. He had not divorced his father; his mother had. She should have allowed him into his life. A bit late for that now. Another mother needed him now. It made him angry to think of it, and he found himself slipping into a retaliatory mood. He did not have to look far for a scapegoat. She was downstairs making demands on him.

It seemed obvious that commitment had to do with mothering. It was not difficult to come to that conclusion, since his father had not been there either for good or bad. He did not think an absentee father could have had much effect on his upbringing, although it would have put a lot of pressure on his mother. It made her more demanding than ever, expecting more of him, like the potential mother downstairs.

He did not know what to do. Something told him to walk away as his father had. He would have liked to have been like his father. Identifying with him would be one way of being close to him, of getting to know him, of being him. But then his baby would be born without a father, just as he had been. Everyone needs a father. He knew that. Was he toying with the idea of penalizing his baby? He could not believe he could even think like that. He was on a merry-go-round. He couldn't wait to jump off it, to run downstairs to tell Miranda how clever she had been in realizing that working things out was so exciting.

ON THE CARDS

TWENTY-ONE-YEAR-OLD Orlando's life was centred on two things. One was women and the other was gambling. He could not see how the two were connected, but since they were the only activities in which he took any interest he thought they had to be. He had intended to go to university, but no subject appealed to him. While his school friends were spending their gap year travelling the world, pulling pints or working as waiters to earn enough to keep them going, Orlando remained at home researching the female body.

He was attractive to his many friends but was becoming less so to his overwhelming mother, a fashion designer, known for her ability to transform unattractive women into attractive ones by sensing what they should wear long before they did. Orlando knew that a university education, even if it included business studies, would not necessarily be an asset were he to join his mother in her business empire. His mother felt that his ability to remember every card in at least two packs did not require further honing. Her preferred option was to get him off her hands. She would fund wherever he wanted to go as long as it was far away and, preferably, he would remain there for a long time. Orlando would often reflect on how ironic it was that throughout his childhood she had put him in the hands of paid carers, but as soon as he showed signs of managing his own life she discouraged him from making any attempt to do so. Orlando wondered whether the control she exercised over how women dressed was nothing more than an extension of the control she exercised over her only child. At the same time, he could not but admire her for caring about how women looked. It was something that was as close to his heart – although not for the same reasons – as it was to hers. One day he hoped she would welcome him into her business.

She was not, of course, the only female designer guru. Several names went back almost a century, and their influence – often during times of social unrest – extended far beyond the world of fashion into politics and social intrigue. Orlando's mother, however, was interested only in image. She wanted men to be attracted to women and to appreciate how they looked. Her interest in men in all other respects was minimal. Orlando was pleased that even the men – many of them gay – who worked with his mother were also concerned that men should be satisfied, even if it was only by a woman.

In one respect he was unlike his mother. While she was concerned with how women looked dressed, he was concerned with how they looked undressed. In other ways he resembled her. He, too, wanted to please women but sometimes wondered if he knew the difference between women like his mother and some gay men.

There had not been a man around in their household for as long as he could remember. He thought it ironic that his only masculine role model was his father who had resented a wife who not only earned more than he did but who spent most of her time away from him. Because her husband's needs were given a low priority, he had made a life for himself elsewhere. Orlando would have liked to have had a man about the house.

Failing that, he tried to convince himself that unlike his mother there might be someone somewhere who if he stayed long enough might want to please him.

He wondered whether in that respect he was not unlike his father. Both of them had wanted his mother to love them. His father had given up on his marriage and left home, but it was clear to Orlando that both his parents had given up on him – his mother in particular by implying that there was no place for him in her business.

Was it men she did not like? For the first time Orlando thought that since he was now an adult perhaps his mother did not really like him either. She had loved him as a child but maybe that was because she could employ others to look after him. It was now a different story. He had asked her to take him into her business, and she had told him to go away.

Was it any wonder that he was so attached to women? Was he trying to make up for something on which he had missed out? He wished there was someone with whom to discuss it, someone with whom he could try and work out what it meant. His friend Carole might be helpful. She revelled in other people's problems. Sitting in a café over a hot chocolate, he realized that he did not know how to begin. Carole was older than he and had a baby. She looked motherly, and just thinking about her made him feel warm and cared for. He wished he had arranged to meet her somewhere less public so that she could demonstrate how she felt about him. He wanted to tell her about his problem, but all he could think of was the dealer at the blackjack table. He had been losing so much lately that the casino had recognized him as a good customer, and at the table they had roped off especially for him he was able to play five hands simultaneously without interruption. He disliked it when he had to wait for others to decide which card to play or when another punter distracted the dealer's attention. He wanted her to be there solely for him. She wore a décolleté that his mother would have hated. Was that why he liked the dealer? He certainly liked it when she leaned forward to scoop up the cards and he caught a glimpse of breasts that had not nurtured him when he really needed them. He could not explain all that to Carole. Instead he took her to the casino so that she could see for herself.

He would *show* her what his problem was. Telling her was too complicated, and anyway his pre-casino buzz was starting. He would combine his two passions. Why had he not thought of it before?

Since he was supporting the casino at the rate of thousands of euros a day, the lobster and vintage Grand Cru with which he plied her meant nothing to the management. It meant very little to him either. He could not wait for her to finish her lunch so that he could play out his fantasies in which there were always two women: one dealing cards on which he fantasized that promises written in invisible ink were being made to him; the other a second woman who stood by his side. She was always there but only for him. He thought of her as the nanny who refused him nothing and always delivered – and, across the table, the mother who promised everything but rarely delivered. Look but don't touch. Maybe the full breasts were intended for him, but they were always out of reach. Day after day he would wait for them to deliver. He wondered how he could have spent so much time and money on such an illusion. What was the point of constantly setting up a situation that could end only in disappointment? He looked at Carole and then at the glass of milk that he always ordered as soon as he began to play. Drinking it for the last time, he looked at his friend and was about to say 'Your place or mine?' when he wondered whether he was ready to give up nannies, too. He looked at her. She was really quite attractive, and she had a small baby. Perhaps he would start tomorrow.

TIM WHITTINGTON

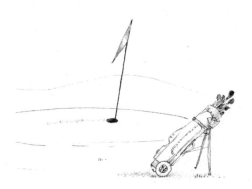

A TERRIBLE THING HAPPENED to Tim. Close to becoming one of the world's great golfers, having almost reached the top of his tree, he suddenly fell off it. He knew why, or thought he did, and tried to convince himself that it was because his wife had been unfaithful. He knew that that was not the real reason, but the truth was too painful. It was not that she had always been a model of rectitude and suddenly was not. She might have cheated on him but not to the extent to which he had cheated on himself.

Stuff happens. But he was unable to reassure himself. It was his own infidelity that bothered him not hers. He would never get over it. The shock of what he had done was too much. He could no longer concentrate on his game, his marriage or his friends.

Normally upright and totally honest, in a single day he lost faith in his integrity and could now no longer trust himself. He had been playing in a minor club competition, having missed the cut in one of the majors a week earlier. He knew how easy it was to become a forgotten man in any sport and was trying desperately hard to prove that his golf was as good as ever.

Perhaps it was that. Even if it was that, it was no excuse. There could never be an excuse.

He was doing quite well, and there should have been nothing else on his mind other than concentrating on his game and keeping his eye on the ball. He was on the par four third, usually an easy birdie, but his second shot had rolled off the back of the green and was a couple of feet into the short grass. It was reasonably close to the pin, and all he needed was a possible chip in for a birdie if he was to claw back a stroke. But then disaster struck. He accidently touched the ball with his club. It moved not more than an inch or two but to a better lie. He did chip in but had never been able to forget that he had written a three on his score card when it should have been a four. His caddy had not noticed because he was lining up a possible putt, and nobody other than he knew about it, but he was terrified that someone might have seen what he had done. Why he had cheated he did not know, but it was essential no one found out. He would never forget it, would never forgive himself, and his golf would never be the same again.

That would have been bad enough, but he had always been a great golfer and had a reputation to maintain. Everyone expected that it would not be long before he hit the golfing headlines again. Everyone who knew him thought that there was a touch of genius about him. How could he explain why he had suddenly gone off his game?

He had been four years old and hitting a golf ball in the garden with a sawn-off club that his father had made for him. The video his proud father had taken of him had been recently shown on television. There had never been a four-year-old to touch him. By the time he was eighteen he was a talented amateur winning a cup in one competition after another. He had always known that he wanted to earn his living playing golf. He loved the game more than anything else. He could not wait until he was old enough to turn pro. When the time came his foot was already in the door. All he had to do was push it open. He loved his club, he loved his golfing companions, he loved the skill and thrill of hitting a great shot, he loved being in the great outdoors in all weathers and he loved competition. He also loved the money he was beginning to earn so that he would be less of a burden to his parents.

It was only recently that he had worked himself up from assistant pro, at the club to which he and his father belonged, to being a recently appointed professional following a string of successes at minor tournaments on his way to bigger things. He was blissfully happy and totally fulfilled until the morning of the disaster. He was now not to be trusted by anyone. There was no question of divorce from the club, or of confession or of asking for forgiveness or even of telling anyone. It was too shameful. He would allow himself to fade into the background because he could not be trusted in the foreground.

But he fell in love and found himself at a level of existence that he had not thought possible. He saw Jan as an angel who had come to save him. Much later, looking back to the day he met her, he remembered it as special and amazing, and a tear would come to his eye whenever he thought of it. She was tall and slim with long black hair, but it was her eyes that were special. They were emerald green, like the fairways after it had been raining. When she looked at him he felt as if she was looking into his soul. He heard her speaking, but he did not know what she was saying. He was not in the here and now but on another planet. She was in the pros' shop to buy a glove, and he knew that his life had changed. Something happened between them that altered everything. He thought that it might even restore him to his former life.

They had previously noticed one another at the club, but nothing other than an occasional greeting had passed between them. As he handed her the glove he felt the slight brush of her fingers. Later he thought of it as similar to seeing a driver and a ball but feeling nothing until they made that magical contact, like his shot off the first tee. This was another touch, another first moment accompanied by speechlessness, embarrassment and longing. Neither of them had known what to do next.

Jan knew she had to say something. It was down to her. It would be too risky to leave it to him. In the moments that had passed she knew intuitively that she was the stronger. She opened her mouth to say something that would ensure continuity. What came out of it was the best she could do.

'Have you had a busy day?' she asked.

Was that enough to prolong the moment, to move their relationship into territory where it could pick up momentum and start a life of its own, enough to impress him with her self-confidence, amaze him with her conversational skills? She had to think of something that demanded more than a yes or no. She tried again.

'I hear you've been doing well in competitions lately.'

He could have muttered something but did not. She was taking an interest. The floodgates were beginning to open.

'I played well at Royal St George last Saturday. I sank a very long putt for an eagle at the eighteenth. Just luck. You might have seen it on Sky.'

'You were brilliant,' she lied. 'We're lucky to have you as our pro.'

She felt a slight unease because truth was important. She added as an afterthought, 'I wish my game was better.'

'I've noticed you on the course. You've got a good swing. All you need is a few lessons.'

He knew he must have been holding his breath because he remembered breathing out. It was not so much a breath as a sigh. Jan knew it was a sigh, and she was happy, and they moved closer not by moving but simply by being.

She had lessons, and rehearsals for their life together began. He put his arms around her under the oak tree on the practice ground, moving her body, altering her stance and changing her grip, and time passed, and in another place she did the same for him. They did not marry under the oak tree, but Tim felt as if they had.

They bought a shop, and while Tim won competitions Jan sold flowers. One day a man pricked his finger on one of her roses, and, returning early from a tournament, Tim found them in bed. Contrite and tearful, he and Jan made it up and tried again. Both wanted it to work. But for Tim everything was a competition. He had to perform better than anyone else – whether it was on the golf course or in bed. He felt at a disadvantage because he knew nothing about his rival, his history, his weaknesses, his strengths, his game plan. Only that he must try harder. One day he tried too hard and failed. He wanted to express his love for her, just as he had wanted to express his love for golf, but he was unable to do so. He knew he was trying too hard and his fear of failure made it worse. He was afraid that Jan might be so distressed by disappointment that she would look for someone else. He was setting up the situation he most dreaded.

He only had two loves in his life. One was his wife and the other was golf. Performance anxiety was affecting both. It was not long before their friends began to recognize that something had gone very wrong.

Standing on the tee at the club one morning with the usual few waiting to play, and at the same time hoping that they would admire his drive, he felt suddenly embarrassed. He did not want anyone watching him. It was his back swing that worried him. He would tell others that getting it up correctly was the key to a good swing, but he was no longer able to do it. He hit a poor shot. It was even worse on the green. He was at least three metres short of the hole after his first putt. 'Never up, never in.' His partner's comments were intended to be helpful, but it was when his putting became affected he finally twigged. Getting it up and getting it in was what golf was all about, what sex was all about, what life was all about and what ultimately his marriage was all about.

Realizing what his problem was began to lift his spirits. It was not his problem. He had not been unfaithful. It was Jan. The fact that his wife had had a slight lapse did not actually worry him in the slightest. It had been his lapse that he thought he would never get over. He told himself that if he failed to perform he had to try harder, but when he tried harder he became increasingly anxious and he failed more often. Everyone was sympathetic. They all knew how emotion could affect their game. He did not mind them knowing. He revelled in their knowing. Jan was a rescuing angel. He loved her all the more. He forgave her and she loved him all the more. In all the best fairy tales the protagonists endure adversity, but all comes right in the end. Their friends were happy, and the world of golf was happy. Tim forgave his wife for her infidelity to him and forgave himself for his infidelity to golf. Putting their sins behind them, they lived happily ever after.

CAUGHT YOU

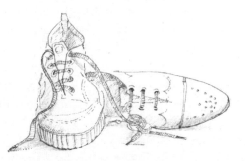

THERE WAS SOMETHING about shoes that John found attractive. Some men were drawn to ties, others to pocket handkerchiefs. He happened to like shoes. He also liked the sensation of his feet being embraced by the softness and pliability of leather. Making television commercials to promote shoe design provided him with work satisfaction. For him there was no 'iron fist in velvet glove' equivalent in the foot. Wearing an elegant, beautifully crafted shoe set aside any possibility of the foot as aggressive. Putting the boot in was not for him. He liked shoes merely as fashion accessories. It pleased him to think that his feet would be protected on his path through life. Shoes, feet, being on the move, not standing still waiting for the world to go by, getting there first, success, winning. It was all of a piece. It was what he wanted. What he thought of. It was his autobiography waiting to be written.

He saw the world as divided into those who thought about where they were going and found time to stand and stare and others who were in a hurry. He was making a plea, through his work, for shoe designers to give more emotional and intellectual credence to life's journey. Beautiful shoes pleased him because he considered their wearers thoughtful, concerned about where they stood and for the paths on which they trod. The carelessly shod were also on their way, but they were not interested in the scenery or their standing. Being on firm ground, the need to feel secure, achievement, moving on, putting down roots was not for everyone.

Shoes were status symbols, and he was in no doubt about where he stood. He would tell anyone who commented on his well-maintained shoes that he believed one could always tell a gentleman by them. What he was likely to be thinking, however, was that one could always tell a lady by how she laced her trainers. They told you everything you needed to know about her. It was not so much about appearance – cleanliness and being in good repair was obviously important – but more about how and why they were worn. He had never been interested in the tightly, and sometimes doubly, laced wearer who had never kicked over the traces because it took her too long to take off her shoes. The loosely laced, one pull and they were off, reflected a temperament that he found more attractive.

But however attractive he found shoes, they shared his thinking with other issues. He considered himself thoughtful and well rounded, although he sometimes wondered whether his earliest childhood attraction to shoes had any significance. Had he used his education and creative talents to gratify a childhood need? That was exactly what he had done. He thought of it as a coincidence but nothing more and told himself that creating a successful commercial was little different from creating a feature film and no less exciting or challenging than promoting other design products in the world in which he lived, toiled and played. But he knew that not to be true. He wished only for those who wore 'his' shoes to be of good standing. But there had always been something else.

He and Daniela, who led the film team in the production company for which he worked, were planning their next project when trainers came into the conversation.

'You're really into shoes,' Daniela said, seeing him eyeing hers.

He could not disagree. Many of his interests were foot-related. His mother, who had called him twinkle toes while he was at school because of his love of ballet, was worried because he had shown more interest than his sister in dancing lessons.

'Got a foot fetish, have we?'

'Rubbish.'

It was more forceful a reply than he intended. It would have been less abrupt had he remembered that it was Daniela to whom he was speaking rather than his mother who years before might well have made – employing other words – a similar comment.

If he did have a fetish it was for the swing music that had kept everyone on their toes in the 1930s. He regarded the world events that had switched the carefree out of their dancing pumps into army boots as one of the ironies of recent history. The fact that he might still be living in his grandparents' past rather than his own, and not moving on, did not occur to him. He knew only that he loved the music of that time and the lyrics that went with it. There was something about the rhythm of the foxtrot, the quickstep, the rumba and the tango. The steps had to be absolutely correct in their timing. It was lyrical poetry, big-band sonnets. He was unsure why he wanted to follow in his grandparents' footsteps, why he still wanted to tiptoe through the past.

Anyway, he liked the word fetish and the feeling it evoked of being irresistibly drawn to the erotic. The word had a ring to it, although he became less enamoured of it when he discovered that someone with a fetish could be potent only in the presence of whatever he associated with sexual arousal. That object acquired a special quality. It did not have to be shoes or feet. It could be anything.

If he did have a fetish it was his work. He had created several short films for one designer. The most recent was for trainers. He had thrown himself into it and had composed the music while Daniela filmed the visuals. A perfect match. The music was as evocative as the visuals, and the storyline was perfect. Even with the visuals off the music delivered the message, although Daniela believed that the message was there without the music. They both thought it their best yet, and there was little more that he could do with it. It was almost right; except for the ending.

He played it through on his iPad. The music was great and the storyline solid, but he did not like the girl wearing the trainers. She did not match the music. Not elegant. Too now. He could not do it with her. That was it. He was unsure what he meant but knew it was a definite no. They were running close to the deadline. Too late for changes. Daniela would have been good. He should have asked her. She was not a model but she was a size five and a half.

Daniela wore the trainers, and they filmed it once more. His black patents chased her pink trainers. Lace-ups but not too tight. Up the stairs and down the corridors. His heart pumping, the music racing; she hiding and he finding. The penultimate shot. One trainer unlaced and on its side, and an elegant bespoke shoe lying close. And, when it seemed all over, the final shot. Pink laces entwined with black. The perfect match. The music had spoken; the shoes had listened and Daniela had said, 'I wouldn't have wanted to be in your shoes if anything had gone wrong.'

IT'S MY BODY

RAISSA WAS NEVER seen without her arms across her chest and her hands tucked under her armpits. Vague thoughts of why she did this crossed her mind. She was aware what it meant and would not forget it. It was too horrible, not something she wanted to think about. Her body would deal with it. This it did by carrying out the ritual without which she felt threatened, unprotected and anxious. It allowed her to face a world that once had terrified her. Occasionally she told herself that what she was doing was a counter-productive habit that served only as a reminder of something that she would like to forget. She could not give it up. If she forced herself to avoid doing it she would have to remain at home. She would be too frightened to go out. She might meet someone who might not like her, someone who could harm her, someone from her days of suffering. What she did was talismanic, a protection against the evil eye. Mentally and physically braced, but always with head bowed and looking to one side, she would stride purposefully forward as if she knew exactly where she was going when, in fact, she had absolutely no idea. No one had ever asked her why she presented herself in this way. She concluded that no one was interested in her. She wanted to be ignored; had no wish to explain. Some might be curious about why she did what she did, curious about what it might mean. They invariably jumped to the wrong conclusions. Her friends, if they really were her friends and not just pretending to be, were sure that not knowing what to do with one's hands, a common enough problem, was likely to be the reason for her idiosyncratic posture. The opinion was that hands were a psychological giveaway and not too difficult to interpret. When the topic arose, always in her absence, they agreed how hands were unlike feet in this respect. It was rare for anyone to worry about what to do with their feet when they were not in use. They always were in use.

Raissa's husband had sometimes considered asking if he might help her with her problem, but he now seldom did so. They discussed it freely, but nothing ever came of it. Raissa had consulted a therapist who helped her to feel better about herself, but the habit persisted. Raoul knew what his wife expected of him, and were he to forget it she would find a way of reminding him. Both of them knew that she did not wish to talk about it.

Raissa's thoughts, when she could bring herself to reflect on them, took her down a different road. She would wonder how women, but seldom men, would settle on a sofa and tuck their feet beneath them, perhaps to protect themselves, like creatures that would roll themselves into balls or encase themselves in their shells when predators were around.

She took the view that feet, constantly involved in activity, were seldom vulnerable to predators other perhaps than on a beach when shoes – other than sandals – were inappropriate. Feet had a role to play, if only for running away. Gloves were out of place indoors; socks were not. While feet served a purpose other than when their owner was standing on them, hands were only in use when they were holding, carrying, concealing or being offered something. They were extended for greeting and for waving farewell. Everyone had something in hand. No one ever had anything in foot. Raissa reflected that the incidence of cancer would be less high if people did not use cigarettes to give them something to do with their hands. She did not smoke and disliked the current equivalent, the mobile phone, as a means of employing hands – although it was what most people did. The mobile phone was antisocial and intrusive. No one would want to listen to anything she had to say. She had nothing to say. She would never have anything to say. What would she use a mobile phone for? To call for help? Who would rescue her? Intimate messages were relayed in public and no one paid attention to what was being said. Were any-one to ask about her body language she had rehearsed her answer. She would tell them that she liked walking with her arms akimbo, well aware that akimbo suggested an aggressive arms-on-hips posture, elbows forwards and perhaps a glare thrown in for emphasis, a posture she would never use. She was far too timid. On the contrary, her posture was self-protective rather than aggressive. Her body language was not just defensive but also rejecting.

On the first morning of the children's summer break, protecting her body, her status, her vulnerability and all her many anxieties, she walked into the dining-room for breakfast in their hotel. As usual she was thinking aggressively but behaving timidly, her postural confusion being an exact reflection of how she dealt with most issues. On the one hand she tried to think of herself as upright, forceful and challenging, but on the other she knew that the opposite was more likely to be correct.

Her body sent messages that were difficult to understand. In akimbo mode she was aggressive, talkative and seemingly indifferent to the feelings of others, but with her arms clasped around her upper body, signalling 'Look after me – I feel vulnerable', no one quite knew how to take her. She complained to Raoul that there were a funny lot of people staying at the hotel this year, meaning that they all seemed to be giving her a bad time.

Sitting at a table she waited to be asked if she wanted coffee or tea. She did not signal this need, and no one responded to it. Catching people's eyes was not a thing she did. Avoidance of eye contact was more usual.

She was aware of a man standing next to her.

'Coffee or tea, madam?'

She turned away. Her mother had told her never to look at the soldiers. Never make eye contact. Always keep your head down. Look away.

Her father's last words were 'They will not notice you. They will leave you alone.'

She had done as he said, but they did notice her, and they did not leave her alone. She remembered suddenly why she always folded her arms across her chest. She was concealing her breasts, hoping they might think she was a boy.

Only a year later, when she met Raoul in the refugee camp, did her life begin its slow journey to something approaching normality. No one except Raoul knew what had happened to her. Fifteen years had passed since the genocide.

She looked at the young man standing patiently beside her and remembered the suffering inflicted on her people by his people. She would not forget it. He would have been no more than three years old at the time. 'Where are you from?' she asked.

He looked puzzled. 'Glasgow. I'm doing a degree course in hotel management. I'm on work experience.'

'Coffee,' she said. 'I'd like a double espresso, please.'

NOLI ME TANGERE

Nick and Lola met on the first day at university. Standing next to one another in a group of freshers waiting to be told what to do next, each sensed the presence of a kindred spirit. It was not long, they thought later, before they realized that whatever it was that passed between them was a moment that was to inform their lives. Looking back, as they did from time to time, at how their lives together had begun they remembered feeling so attuned that it was as if each of them had, in some magical way, become the other. Despite this emotional closeness, or maybe because of it, their relationship remained platonic. They did not regard this as unusual, and neither of them seemed troubled by it.

By the end of the first term they were struggling to keep up with the lectures. It was not that the course they had chosen was beyond them but that they felt themselves being drawn to other areas of interest that they had not previously considered. They decided – and their tutors agreed – that they had made a mistake in thinking that history was for them and that choosing a subject more in keeping with their mindsets would be the right thing to do.

It was not the historical past to which they were drawn but their own. Theatre interested them more. What took longer for them to recognize was that it was not so much theatre that attracted them but theatricality. They both thought they had found what they were looking for at the drama society. The idea of representing themselves as someone they were not, speaking words written for anyone who cared to use them, wearing clothes chosen by a wardrobe mistress and behaving not as they might wish but as the director instructed took them into a world hitherto unknown but one in which they immediately felt at home.

Lola and Nick left university and completed a two-year course at drama school aimed at training them for professional work in the theatre. There they found like-minded others whose desire to be looked at and admired matched their own. They discovered that each of them had a 'look but don't touch' attitude of which they had previously been unaware.

After graduation the pair joined a repertory company where every working day was a life-enhancing experience. An actress in whom they confided said she felt the same and described the feeling as sexual. Nick and Lola continued to spend almost every moment of their lives together. Whatever emotional needs they had were satisfied not so much by one another but by the audience's appreciation of their efforts to please. Apart from their fellow actors, whom they thought of as family, there were no others in their lives. They were members of a team. They had learned their acting skills as a team and looked forward to continuing as a team. Each night, as the lights dimmed and the audience disappeared, they evolved from who they had been into who they were. It was a long time before they realized that their two personae were the same. Their work filled and fulfilled their lives. They had no need for anything other than the roles, which took them not out of themselves but into themselves. They were drunk with the satisfaction brought by the characters they played and the audience's reaction to them. They could wish for nothing more.

Nick was the first to break away from a pattern that was now a comfortable routine. He explained to Lola that the time had come for him to do something that was more stimulating. That something was illusion.

'I've been practising,' he said, 'and I think I'm quite good.'

He had been doing party tricks ever since Lola had known him, but it had not occurred to her that he might want to earn his living doing them.

'I need my audience to work out what's going on,' Nick said. 'To make an effort to know me better, to be closer. I want to entertain them.' He wanted them not just to like him but to study him more closely. He did not say that because he assumed Lola would know.

There was a silence while they thought about the changes Nick was considering. Nick wondered why he had said that being entertaining would bring people closer. The word 'entertain' triggered a memory of his mother taking him to a neighbour's birthday party and telling him that everyone would be required to perform after tea. 'But I can't sing or do anything,' he had told her. He remembered it very clearly. The others would like him, she had told him, if he performed well. Would they not like him if he could not perform? Did he still feel that? Would he always have to sing for his supper to be accepted? Was appearance everything?

Lola thought that this was as good a time as any to tell him what she had in mind. 'I'm not surprised,' she said, 'that we've both come up with the need to change at the same time. That's how it has always been with us. I've been thinking. I like the idea of pole-dancing. It would ensure that the audience pays attention. I would like us to stay in partnership, and although we will be separate we will be billed as a double act. That way we can please everyone.' She did not tell Nick that for as long as she could remember she had fantasized about offering a man something for which he had an overwhelming desire. But denying him any possibility of having it would make the term 'happy at work' an understatement. Her thoughts flickered, not for the first time, over why the concept of disappointment, of looking but not having, was so pleasurable. She would have loved to know.

There had been a silence while they each wondered what the other had in mind. They were unsure what was in their own minds but knew that such a change in lifestyle must signal something important. Neither of them liked change, but both knew that what they had discussed was something they wanted to do, something they were drawn to. For weeks they tried not thinking about it, but it was not long before they appeared on the bill as a double act at a club in the centre of the city.

Their first day came, and Nick, billed as a member of the Magic Circle, started the ball rolling. It soon became clear that the audience, mainly men, was not interested in magic. They had come to see pole-dancing. They talked over him while he did his best to entertain them and waited impatiently for Lola to appear. They knew the rules. Look but don't touch. The applause was overwhelming. Lola had always enjoyed being looked at, but this was different. She had found herself, and she had found her sexuality. She had discovered why she and Nick had never had physical contact with one another. He had never looked at her, and she had never looked at him. They both enjoyed being looked at, and that had seemed enough. Night after night the audience more or less booed Nick off the stage.

At the end of their three-month trial Nick shook hands with Lola, and their life together came to an end as suddenly as it had started. It had taken them a long time to become wiser.

'What a pity it is', Lola said, 'that neither of us is a voyeur.'

Nick left the room wondering whether she would be impressed with the coin he had magicked from her ear. She smiled, sadly he thought, but did not look up.

BUSY BODY

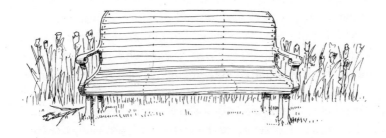

WILLIAM BELIEVED IN social correctness, by which he meant the right of everyone to go about free from interference and free from those who, with little sense of community, contaminated and abused the environment. At a time when atmospheric pollution was approaching danger level, respiratory problems on the increase and litter everywhere, he considered it his duty to remind drivers of stationary cars to switch off their engines, to instruct those with feet on train or bus seats to consider the effect on others and to insist that litterers pick up their rubbish and dispose of it in an appropriate bin. A self-appointed vigilante in men's lavatories he commented loudly when handwashing was neglected and regretted only that custom prevented him from doing the same in women's washrooms.

Walking to the bus stop with his friend Donald, after lunch with seven other retired police officers, he thought about a topic they had discussed on which all had had strong views. It was the increase not in road accidents caused by motorists behaving badly but in pavement accidents caused by cyclists behaving badly. William knew what they thought about bad behaviour in general, much of which crossed their paths even after their retirement, but not what they thought about the behaviour of errant cyclists.

It had been years since they had left their posts, their cars and their drivers and found themselves once again waiting at bus stops and supermarket check-outs. It was ironic that the relatively minor problems that during their working lives they had left others to address – on the grounds that there were more important matters with which they had to deal – they were now being forced to confront themselves. The small coterie who had talked and worked together for years and were still talking together in their retirement (and would probably continue to do so in the afterlife) had formed themselves into a male luncheon club which their wives regarded as a meeting of vigilantes. They met once a month for debates about the social ills of the moment and for the airing of personal prejudices. They were as interested in bad behaviour, whether antisocial or criminal, as they had been throughout their working lives. Their views ranged from the draconian to the lenient on how best to deal with behavioural problems. Their debates brought them closer to the core of their prejudices, but increased their frustrations at their inability to deal with them in an appropriate manner.

As former guardians of the law they knew the difference between right and wrong but seemed less concerned about the difference between right and further right. They would have denied bigotry in their discussions, but their opinions were often informed by a certain unyielding attitude when it came to the misdeeds of others and the need to air their intolerances.

One of these was gender-related. It was not that they did not like women. They were all married and dependent on the care provided by their partners. None the less, their meetings were men only. Women, they agreed, did not think like men, did not behave like men and were ill-fitted to talk about the issues that preoccupied men. This view was based on the fact that women rarely, if ever, told jokes, and if they did they were seldom funny – not a particularly valid reason for their exclusion perhaps but one that was referred to when the gender issue came up. Soon after they had retired and had decided that it was important to keep in touch with their friends and from time to time enjoy a meal with them, one spouse had asked whether she might join them. She had been told by her husband that he had never been invited to a hen party and politely asked her why she had enquired.

They all demonstrated politically incorrect attitudes about almost everything including gay rights, race, religion and multiculturalism. Although such topics were occasionally mentioned or discussed they did not believe they were anything other than liberal intellectuals who knew how to conduct themselves. They would have been mortified if anyone had suggested that they sometimes came across as right-wing bigots. They looked forward to their meetings and thoroughly enjoyed sharing their opinions on how to run the country or deal with issues, political or social, about which they might from time to time feel strongly. There was no shortage of issues to discuss or injustices to put right. When the conversation turned to crime and punishment, as it frequently did, they were at one. They were unaware that their partners looked forward to their meetings as much as they did and would quote the timeworn adage that women married their partners for life but not for lunch. None of them believed this for a moment and thought of it as a not particularly amusing joke.

On their way to the bus stop Donald and William decided to make a minor diversion into the park. Having eaten neither wisely nor particularly well they began to speak of problems they had not been able to address at lunch by virtue of the seating arrangements. Donald was not, in fact, a policeman – he had spent his working life employed as an accountant in charge of the police payroll – but he was an unofficial adviser on business affairs to any of the others who cared to consult him. They liked Donald and regarded him as a guru who was never short of information and a concern for the group's well-being. Their only complaint was that although Donald had booked the table he had forgotten the importance of requesting a circular table to facilitate collective debate. They had spent an exhausting two hours having shouted conversations with those sitting at opposite ends of a long one.

William had opened the meeting with the 'cycling on the pavement' issue. They had talked about it before, but their views had been varied, and he was interested to find out whether they still felt the same way about what he considered a major irritant.

'It has to stop. It's becoming too dangerous. I was nearly knocked down on the way here.' They all had views about the matter, but the consensus was that the authorities were to blame for not having made proper provision for cyclists in the first place.

Hubert, a former Chief Inspector, thought that the mayor's initiative of providing cycles to rent at strategic points so that people could leave their cars at home was a good one. William's view was that in some areas they were used mainly by tourists, who wearing neither helmets nor protective clothing had no idea where they were going and tended to wobble while trying to read street names. This all added to the danger, especially when they concluded that the bad behaviour of native cyclists was also unacceptable. What worried William was that Hubert had gone on to say that he preferred cyclists to ride on pavements because at least they would not be at risk of being crushed by a left-turning bus. This was despite William's insistence that how cyclists rode their bicycles was their own responsibility and that they had chosen to take whatever the risks were. It could not, he said, be compared with the risk to pedestrians.

William was still clearly upset by the comments of someone whose job it had been to enforce the law, who in his retirement was taking a view that put the law in disrepute and who was sitting too far away for him to deal with quietly and diplomatically. They had reached the park, and it was a warm day for the end of March. They were tired, and there were still matters to talk about for which they had not had time at lunch. Sitting on the nearest seat from where they could see the budding daffodils and the trees with pale-green leaf buds waiting for a few more hours of warm sunshine before they declared themselves, they were surprised to see a young man pick the heads off a few of the flowers and place them decoratively behind his ears. They were unsure what to do. Concerned that the flowers in the park were for the benefit of everyone, they felt it their duty to point this out. The young man looked bewildered. He was obviously from South-East Asia rather than south-east London, and when William addressed him he smiled agreeably and handed him a daffodil. William nodded his head politely to show his appreciation, and the young man replied by bowing deeply. This caused the flowers he had so carefully placed behind his ears to fall to the ground. Because he seemed upset, William, who felt some responsibility for what had happened, helped him gather them up.

He wondered for the first time whether there might possibly be a place for 'live and let live', not only in the world, the integrity of which he spent so much effort trying to preserve but in his thinking. It would certainly reduce the need to shout the next time Donald forgot to book a round table. They could choose a different topic. Hot air and rubbish might be a good place to start. There was a lot of it about.

SEXPLOITATION

CATHIE AND JOHN managed their arm's-length relationship in a way that suited them. Cathie had been attracted to John as soon as she met him and within a day or two had used her timeworn method to test his suitability as a possible life partner – by having sex with him. John was a willing collaborator. His philosophy was to accept whatever sexual activity was on offer, since his relationships were based on eroticism more than affection. Meeting twice a week, they told one another that they would have liked their 'encounters' – a term that described their meetings well – to be more frequent but that the pattern suited them. When they were apart they spent their time Skyping or texting, neither realizing why distanced intimacy appealed to them. When Cathie thought of what it was that made their liaison attractive, she told herself that, for as long as she could remember, she had been used to the idea of relationships being neither close nor long lasting. She believed that to be her mother's view also, since they had both been left without a man in the house when her father fell in love with another woman. She had been four years old at the time, but it had never occurred to her that her mother was not alone in holding the opinion that men were not the only ones incapable of forming a loving relationship. She would have liked to describe her encounters with men as more than just physical but acknowledged that at least they were sexual encounters with a view.

She would have liked to think that it was because her work as a journalist took up most of her time but knew that it was not the real reason. Alone in her bed at night she fantasized about her detached relationship with John, trying to convince herself that his protestations of love, the places they visited and their walks in the countryside were what she enjoyed most. But what she really took pleasure in was not so much the sex – although she tried to persuade herself to the contrary – but her insistence on encouraging him to buy smart clothes and have his hair cut so that he would look exactly as she wanted him to. It did not occur to either of them that she was unable to accept him as he was or that anything short of a makeover would put their end-game into play. He was her doll, her toy, her playmate but also someone, her past experience told her, she would grow out of. She was unaware that she might be trying to recreate an image of someone buried in the depths of her memory but lost to her for ever.

Psychologically intrusive and pathologically untrustworthy, she used his pillow talk, confessions in which he was least able to keep some of his more erotic needs to himself, as source material for her weekly column. He is using me, so why should I not use him? she asked herself when her condemning conscience sought to reproach her. All I'm doing is making him pay back what I gave him in the first place; loving concern he will probably use one day with another woman, at another time, in another place. Women always give and men always take. It's normal. Hacking into his thinking was no worse than reporters hacking into the emails of celebrities in the interests of their readership. Justice was being done, she told herself, despite being certain that it was not.

John became even more adventurous during their sexual encounters. Although seemingly enjoying their lovemaking, he appeared lost in his own world, in which Cathie seemed not to belong or from which she had been excluded. His daydreams, a few of which he discussed, were unlike anything with which she was familiar. Her own fantasies were self-seeking, controlling, ultimately selfish and usually about wealth and power. John's were erotic and involved faceless women whose role was to gratify him. Those with their own needs featured nowhere in his thinking. His ambition was to act out his fantasies with Cathie. Those he was unable to re-enact with her – they were either too violent or too dangerous – remained the substance of his thoughts and gratified him only when he was alone. Unlike Cathie, he was uninterested in the pursuit of affection, but, like her, he was on the look-out for an opportunity to redeem what he thought life owed him.

It was not long before each of them discovered that they were mirror images of one another. Their tastes and interests were identical. They liked the same colours, the same leisure activities and the same food. They were hooked on cold fish because they were cold fish. Sheltering within the shell of the crabs and lobsters that were a feature of their meals together, they believed they were loving and gentle, but as far as physical contact went it were their claws with which they caressed each other.

Each of them loved the cinema. In the darkness of the auditorium, with the projector behind them and the screen in front of them, they were able for a while, through the suspension of disbelief, to feel happily enclosed within a womb-like anxiety-free environment. They were temporary inhabitants of a fairy tale in which the protagonists either lived happily ever after – an illusion in which neither of them had any faith – or killed one another to satisfy wishes for revenge engendered by their parents. They did not care for violence. It was too close to home. It was innuendo, the playful yet essentially hostile put-downs of comedies, that tuned into their fantasies.

Cathie convinced herself that she enjoyed their weekly meetings. But there was something about their afternoons together that made her apprehensive. She could not dismiss from her mind John's insistence on repeating activities reminiscent of his time in the nursery, and although she told herself frequently that she loved him she was not always able to avoid disagreeable demands – based on images from his remote past – that came between them. She wondered whether she would feel the same with other men and thought that she probably would.

Eventually John's insistence that she please him, despite her occasional reluctance to re-enact his nursery needs, empowered her. His passivity concerning her own needs and his craving for attention frightened her. She wondered increasingly often why his needs were so insatiable and why he seldom found it necessary to satisfy hers. She sensed that he was punishing her for being the cold fish to which he was paradoxically attracted because his mother might also have been one. Insights into his thoughts gave her the strength to examine their relationship more closely. Although she did whatever he asked of her, she began to realize that one day, when the novelty faded, he would leave her. And if he did not, because he had failed her sex test she would leave him, a situation she knew she would be unable to avoid setting up. They were doomed. Neither she nor anyone else would be able to compensate him for what he was looking for, any more than he would be able to compensate her for what she sought.

As they began to tire of the sameness of one another, Cathie wondered whether her horizons were widening as emotional truths and understanding of her repetitive behaviour were beginning to surface. She made a decision. She would approach relationships with men differently. She would reserve intimate involvement only for when she was sure she had found a man who was as kind and concerned for her well-being as she hoped she would be for his. She would not use sex as a calling card to assess attraction. Nor would she use it as a vehicle to return to a past that had been unsatisfactory in the first place and which her recent experience was beginning to tell her would be just as unsatisfactory in any other place. Her future might be less bleak, something to which to look forward rather than back. She concluded that appetite satisfaction was fine but that a liaison in which both partners looked less for what was on offer and more for what they could contribute was preferable. They would continue on a road well travelled but they would encourage the future to beckon rather than the past.

DAMNED SPOT

IT WAS EARLY morning and still cold. Teddy sat in the kitchen of the family home watching his mother prepare breakfast. He was pleased that she had given up dreams of nursing for marriage to a house.

He had no idea that it was more his mother's timidity, her lack of self-confidence and her fear that she had not been a good enough mother that kept her attending to the emotional and physical needs of her three sons when she should have been encouraging them to grow up and leave home.

Teddy liked to think it was her concern for his well-being that kept her tied to their home little more than a mile away from a motorway that would, should she have wanted to use it, transport her to whatever was on offer in the city. The reason for her decision was known only to the social services. They had been called in when his father had turned from mentally abusing his wife to doing the same to Teddy.

His mother had never abandoned her belief that she had failed to protect her four-year-old when his father had been accused of ill-treating him. She was convinced that Teddy still needed her, even to the extent of getting up early and cooking his breakfast. Teddy, however, had no recollection of his father's hostility, although he was aware that he did not particularly like him. His mother's protectiveness compensated him both for being the youngest child as well as being the one his father cared for least. It strengthened their liaison.

Teddy was happy that his mother insisted on sending him off to work with a good breakfast and a goodbye kiss – as if he were still a schoolboy – when an early start was needed on the small-holding that was all that was left of the family farm. He would remain her baby for as long as he needed her and as long as she needed him. Their codependency compensated for his mother's inability to cope with his opinionated, controlling and sometimes violent father.

Teddy idolized his two older brothers and longed to be like them, but he knew that he had a long way to go before he caught up with their self-assurance. He was not academic, had no idea about what he wanted from life, lacked ambition and felt that growing up and making his own way in the world was too daunting even to think about. His father showed little interest in his problems other than being irritated by them, but both mother and son accepted his immaturity, not least because it held them together.

Teddy made his usual half-hearted protest about being quite capable of getting himself off to work. He had told his mother the night before that he had a particularly pressing job to do, but she still pretended that he was incapable of getting his own breakfast. She knew that he was perfectly capable of cooking, but it was her duty to do it for him, and anyway it made her feel better with herself when her maternal role was fulfilled.

Unlike his brothers Teddy had not lived up to his father's expectations. He was too young to understand that his father's own lack of achievement insisted that he relive his life through his sons. His father took pride in his older brothers but clearly not in him. Colin was at university studying mathematics, and Robert spent most of his time with his girlfriend. Teddy regarded his older brothers as heroes for managing to break away from the tyrannical restraints imposed on all of them by their father, whose resentment that none of his sons was interested in dragging his grandparents' dairy farm into the twenty-first century – a step he had himself failed to achieve – hung over them like a dark shadow.

Robert had chosen that evening to announce he would finally be moving out. He had not picked his time well. He had reckoned on his mother being tolerant of his proposal, but he dreaded what his father's reaction might be. Dinner was over, and permission was about to be given for them to leave the table. His father was tired and more than usually irritable. He had, as ever, controlled the dinner-time conversation, talking loudly over any comment volunteered by his sons with which he did not agree. He had been engaged in a monologue concerning a taxation system that he was convinced penalized the country's industry unfairly and had drunk himself into such a state that Robert thought him not only incapable of taking in his news but too far gone to care about it.

'Father, I've got something to tell you.'

'What?'

Robert dropped his bombshell. 'It's about Margaret.'

'Well?' He stared at his oldest son with suspicion. Teddy began to feel nervous. His father, who only a moment before had seemed virtually comatose, was now belligerent. Robert paused, not so much for effect but because his mouth had become dry.

'She wants me to move in with her.'

In rehearsing this moment Robert had naïvely deluded himself into believing that a man-to-man approach, with its suggestion of adult responsibility, would impress his father. But, as far as his father was concerned, there was room for only one man in the family, and he was certainly not Robert. Even Teddy, with his lack of experience, thought that there must have been a better way for his brother to have broken the news than to have come out with it so boldly, but none of them was prepared for the violent rage with which the announcement was greeted. Holding his shaking glass in his hand, their father lurched to his feet, spilling down the front of his white shirt the claret that he insisted his family drink rather than the Heineken they all preferred. Whenever Teddy recalled the incident, he could remember only a red stain spreading across his father's chest. As time passed he forgot what the row had been about, but he never forgot the image of his father slumped over the table looking as if his brother had shot him. Why it remained as vivid as it had been on that fateful evening was something he never understood.

PULL YOURSELF TOGETHER

AS HEAD OF a day centre responsible for the care of infants left by mothers whose lifestyle required that they juggle their reproductive imperatives with equally pressing demands made upon them by family economics, Tessa had a problem with which she needed help. It had to do with babies, but it differed from the mothers' concerns at the day centre. She had no need for anyone to look after her baby while she was at work, because she did not have a baby. It had to do with her desire not to become pregnant.

Her mother, had she been alive, would have been the obvious person to talk to. Tessa knew that not all girls found it easy to discuss issues with their mother, but while she was growing up her own mother's advice, although predictable, was always helpful. Her mother had not approved of children having problems because they would become distressed by them, and distress was disruptive, noisy and a weakness. In her book, children were expected to deal with problems by either 'pulling themselves together' or, as they became older, being told to 'get over it'. Another of her mother's upbringing mantras was to 'do as I tell you'. Her directives – and they were many – were inscribed both upon Tessa's childhood and upon her psyche. They would have extended beyond the grave if her mother had given any thought to what she wanted written on her tombstone.

Tessa had occasional doubts about whether her mother's child-rearing methods had anything going for them. She suspected, but was not entirely certain, that denying the existence of a problem did not always cause it to go away. She had wondered whether her current predicament could be a leftover from childhood reappearing as something else, but it distressed her that her mother was not there to put her stamp upon it.

Her problem had to do with her boyfriend. They had been going out for a year, loved one another and had agreed to marry. But there was a fly in the ointment of their content-ment. Bob wanted children and Tessa did not. They had discussed it *ad nauseam* and got absolutely nowhere. Each of them was as entrenched as the other in attitudes they believed were conditioned in them by their upbringing, and neither of them would, nor probably could, budge an inch.

All Tessa could do was reflect on what had been drummed into her in a childhood that seemed to have gone on for longer than anyone else's and which was probably still affecting her thinking. Not that she minded. Her mother had always been categorical. She would either have sorted out her problem or dismissed it. Tessa would then have been able to stop worrying about it.

There were several other issues she wanted to discuss with Bob, but there was never enough time. Whether they were entirely compatible. Whether their early life experiences would weigh too heavily upon their future. How she really enjoyed ensuring that mothers – obviously concerned about the well-being of their infants left in her care – had confidence in her ability to look after their children. How she kept babies in their familiar routine, providing them with the food to which they were accustomed and calming them when they were tearful. She was at home with all of that but never told Bob that sometimes she saw her mother in how she thought of her charges. She never told them to pull themselves together if anything upset them even though she was sometimes tempted to do so.

Bob also wanted to speak of family life and of their future together. He loved children and in his mother's eyes had been a blue-eyed boy who could do no wrong. He could not wait to relive the joys of his upbringing with a blue-eyed wunderkind of his own. Tessa wanted to rewrite his childhood indoctrination, and he wanted to rewrite hers. She was interested in babies, but was it only in other people's babies? If only Bob could understand that her main concern was to obey her mother's injunctions. Her mother had never approved of dithering. But would she be telling Tessa to have a baby or not to have a baby or just telling her to pull herself together?

She saw a woman leaving the supermarket with a carrier bag on which was printed 'I'm strong. I'm sturdy'. What did it mean? Surely it was intended to impress customers with the quality and strength of the bag. There was nothing wrong with that. But it had a curious effect on her and reminded her of the slogans imprinted on her childhood. Was her mother keeping an eye on her? Did she think she had forgotten her words of wisdom? Could she still be manipulating her thinking? There was no 'pull yourself together' message on her mother's tombstone. She had sent her a message on a supermarket bag instead. She was simply amazing. Tessa knew exactly what she had to do.

SOME AUTHORS WE HAVE PUBLISHED

James Agee • Bella Akhmadulina • Tariq Ali • Kenneth Allsop • Alfred Andersch
Guillaume Apollinaire • Machado de Assis • Miguel Angel Asturias • Duke of Bedford
Oliver Bernard • Thomas Blackburn • Jane Bowles • Paul Bowles • Richard Bradford
Ilse, Countess von Bredow • Lenny Bruce • Finn Carling • Blaise Cendrars • Marc Chagall
Giorgio de Chirico • Uno Chiyo • Hugo Claus • Jean Cocteau • Albert Cohen
Colette • Ithell Colquhoun • Richard Corson • Benedetto Croce • Margaret Crosland
e.e. cummings • Stig Dalager • Salvador Dalí • Osamu Dazai • Anita Desai
Charles Dickens • Bernard Diederich • Fabián Dobles • William Donaldson
Autran Dourado • Yuri Druzhnikov • Lawrence Durrell • Isabelle Eberhardt
Sergei Eisenstein • Shusaku Endo • Erté • Knut Faldbakken • Ida Fink
Wolfgang George Fischer • Nicholas Freeling • Philip Freund • Dennis Friedman
Carlo Emilio Gadda • Rhea Galanaki • Salvador Garmendia • Michel Gauquelin
André Gide • Natalia Ginzburg • Jean Giono • Geoffrey Gorer • William Goyen
Julien Gracq • Sue Grafton • Robert Graves • Angela Green • Julien Green
George Grosz • Barbara Hardy • H.D. • Rayner Heppenstall • David Herbert
Gustaw Herling • Hermann Hesse • Shere Hite • Stewart Home • Abdullah Hussein
King Hussein of Jordan • Ruth Inglis • Grace Ingoldby • Yasushi Inoue
Hans Henny Jahnn • Karl Jaspers • Takeshi Kaiko • Jaan Kaplinski • Anna Kavan
Yasunuri Kawabata • Nikos Kazantzakis • Orhan Kemal • Christer Kihlman
James Kirkup • Paul Klee • James Laughlin • Patricia Laurent • Violette Leduc
Lee Seung-U • Vernon Lee • József Lengyel • Robert Liddell • Francisco García Lorca
Moura Lympany • Dacia Maraini • Marcel Marceau • André Maurois
Henri Michaux • Henry Miller • Miranda Miller • Marga Minco • Yukio Mishima
Quim Monzó • Margaret Morris • Angus Wolfe Murray • Atle Næss • Gérard de Nerval
Anaïs Nin • Yoko Ono • Uri Orlev • Wendy Owen • Arto Paasilinna • Marco Pallis
Oscar Parland • Boris Pasternak • Cesare Pavese • Milorad Pavic • Octavio Paz
Mervyn Peake • Carlos Pedretti • Dame Margery Perham • Graciliano Ramos
Jeremy Reed • Rodrigo Rey Rosa • Joseph Roth • Ken Russell • Marquis de Sade
Cora Sandel • George Santayana • May Sarton • Jean-Paul Sartre
Ferdinand de Saussure • Gerald Scarfe • Albert Schweitzer • George Bernard Shaw
Isaac Bashevis Singer • Patwant Singh • Edith Sitwell • Suzanne St Albans • Stevie Smith
C.P. Snow • Bengt Söderbergh • Vladimir Soloukhin • Natsume Soseki • Muriel Spark
Gertrude Stein • Bram Stoker • August Strindberg • Rabindranath Tagore
Tambimuttu • Elisabeth Russell Taylor • Emma Tennant • Anne Tibble • Roland Topor
Miloš Urban • Anne Valery • Peter Vansittart • José J. Veiga • Tarjei Vesaas
Noel Virtue • Max Weber • Edith Wharton • William Carlos Williams • Phyllis Willmott
G. Peter Winnington • Monique Wittig • A.B. Yehoshua • Marguerite Young
Fakhar Zaman • Alexander Zinoviev • Emile Zola